WORLD PEACE

OF GLORY AND SENSES

MAGIC MASON

Copyright © 2024 by Magic Mason

All rights reserved. This book or any of its portion may not be reproduced or transmitted in any means, electronic or mechanical, including recording, photocopying, or by any information storage and retrieval system, without the prior written permission of the copyright holder except in the case of brief quotations embodied in critical reviews and other noncommercial uses permitted by copyright law.

Printed in the United States of America
Library of Congress Control Number: 2024924484
ISBN: Softcover 979-8-89518-515-5
       e-Book   979-8-89518-517-9
       Hardback 979-8-89518-516-2
Published by: WP Lighthouse
Publication Date: 11/21/2024

To buy a copy of this book, please contact:
WP Lighthouse
Phone: +1-888-668-2459
support@wplighthouse.com
wplighthouse.com

LEGAL CONCEPTS OF LAW AND HUMAN BEHAVIOR SENSES AND CAP ECONOMY

MAJID KHODABANDEH

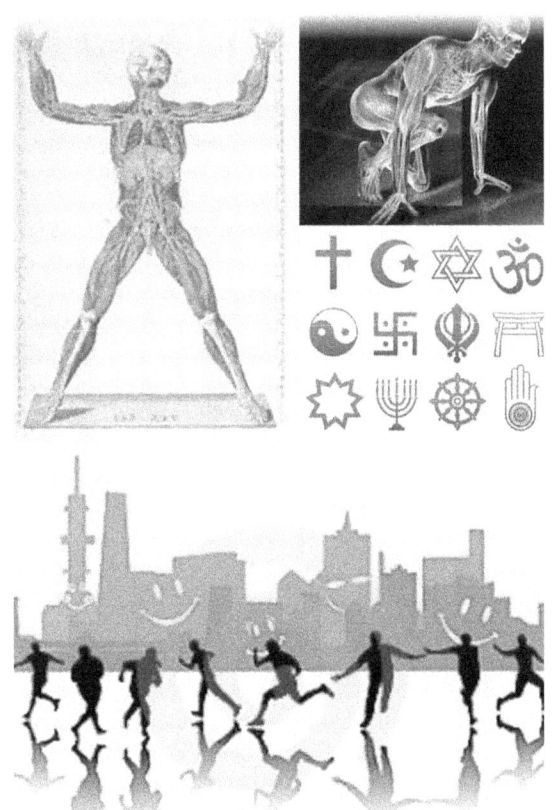

CONTENTS

LEGAL CONCEPTS OF LAW AND HUMAN BEHAVIOR SENSES 1
ABOUT THE AUTHOR 2
BUILD A HUMAN FREEDOM 2
HUMAN THINKER 3
INDUSTRIAL REVOLUTION 6
9 SENSES 8
HOLES IN BODY 10
EARLY CHILDHOOD 11
CHILDHOOD AND 9 SENSES 12
HUMAN HAS 9 SENSES 14
DISCOVERY OF HUMAN SENSES 15
SENSE OF 9TH 16
MIDDLE CHILDHOOD 17
ADULTHOOD 18
EDUCATION ON GENERAL 22
CULTURAL DIFFERENCES 24
GENERAL PSYCHOLOGY OF HUMAN 25
LEGAL CONCEPTS OF LAW AND HUMAN BEHAVIOR SENSES. 28
PSYCHOLOGY BASED ON HUMAN HAS 9 29

LEGAL CONCEPTS OF LAW AND HUMAN BEHAVIOR SENSES

•Law – rules regulations laid down by the state and backed up by enforcement. Society requires laws in order to protect the populace and ensure people live peacefully with one another. The history of laws and lawmaking as well as how they impact religion and psychology, goes back to ancient times as seen in writings by Socrates, Plato, Homer, and others. Majid khodabandeh in this book traces the origins of laws and how law has directly affected the world and the way society understand relations through his worldwide travels and has been seen how laws contribute and protect the populace and hopes one day humanity will be improved by better laws and strong societal vision.

ABOUT THE AUTHOR
MAJID KHODABANDEH

- Majid Khodabandeh was born in Tehran, Iran, U.S. Citizen with diverse international experience. Doctor of
- Philosophy, General Psychology in progress. Master of Public Administration, Bachelor of Science in Industrial
- Technology and Construction Management, from Northern Kentucky University.
- Business Owner, Greater Cincinnati area, 2004- 2015.
- - Author/ Inventor, Legal Concept of the Law and Human Behavior Senses. Amazon. com Published 2009.
- - World Language, published . Amazon. Com 2017
- - Invented political Chess Game: an expansion of classic chess designed to help children learn about political systems. (patent, 2006).
- - Created " super Bed" to reduce heating and cooling expenses.(patent, 2009).

BUILD A HUMAN FREEDOM

LEGAL CONCEPTS " LAW"

• Law made up of rules and regulations, laid down by the state and backed up by enforcement. In everyday life with too many things around us we needed to live peacefully next to each other, to environment and nature we needed some laws and regulations that can protect us or privacy, property, provide safety to all, in city and work places, building good structure and following building codes , safety for our incant children, all right for handicaps and senior citizen, protect innovation and inventors and writers with freedom, also freedom of any racial or civil laws and bad behaviors or violence and solve the mental and health issue in society.

LEGAL CONCEPTS " LAW"

• How can civil laws or criminal laws can judge and protect the citizen. What is different among federal, state, and local laws. My focus of this book is to introduce the history of laws in past and present and how must be write laws for future. How with laws can change the person or society, or family or organization or even world. Today's we need more humanity laws than before to live peacefully.

LEGAL CONCEPTS "LAW"

- History offers numerous illustrations of importance avoidances and counsel in all over the world during times. Using laws and management tools to process of human activity and behaviors.
- Works of such thinkers as Homer, Plato, Hanfeizu, Skrattes, Francis Bacon, Abneh Sina, Boghrath as well as the teaching of prophets like Moses, Jesus, and Mohammad convey the vision of that process in the past and lay the ground work for creating a laws and managerial systems for psychology and behaviors of human being.

HUMAN THINKER
STARTING POINTS OF LAWS

- In order to create a new laws management must be capable to addressing the future of our freedom with safety and comfort for humans. With a good laws management or leaders can be good concepts and techniques. Of course, those laws were not born in twenty first century and all process of experience and past wrongdoing or past lack of information.
- Starting point for laws was the stone age- the prehistoric Era 10,000- 9,000 BC, where within the family unit laws emerged.

STARTING POINTS OF LAWS

- After many years pass of humanity later unexpended as tribal managers were sought for advice and provide laws on family or hunting's and protection from animals and enemy attacks. Tribal gathering or visiting with meeting with wise man or family, friends, neighbors. The small villages grew and become more civilized. Development of civilization with laws and management grow during times. The traditional manager or fathers become kings, priests, and ministers which was leaders who controlled the power and wealth of society with word of wisdom which becomes laws.
- The managerial rules and laws are used in early Egyptian society and still used in some countries governed by kings.

GREEK CIVILIZATION

HISTORY OF LAWS

• Faulty information about past civilization has continually misdirected human being, men, women, and children, misinterpretation and lack of information in past time of Moses, Jesus, and Mohammad with holy books Tora , Bible and Koran, passed information wrong generation to generation through oral traditions or written for example 10 commands or society laws and rules in that 10 commands or laws. If I said in today's world with too many religious leaders we must know basic .If we say everybody must follow Moses 10 commands If I am raciest or basically I don't have common senses to don't kill or don't do adultery or lie is only Moses said so, If it is right to say just Moses said so.

EGYPTIAN CIVILIZATION

HISTORY OF LAWS

• Old Testament Koran in Geneses have different views of laws for instance the story of creation of Adam and Eve have implied in cestuses relationships between father and his children mother with his son sibling's as means of populating the world. Another example is the story of Noah prophet and story of world Flooded. According to scripture the entire world was covered by water as a result of God's wrath toward men wicked habits and Noah and his immediate family being sole survivors of the catastrophe. It is important to consider that story refers to the world as it was known at the time. It was not yet known if the world was flat or round- thousands of years before the discovery of America.

HISTORY OF LAWS

• Galileo and discovery of world was almost 500 years ago. We know church punished Galileo for his discovery and church said he was crazy, and they said world is not round and they don't go around a sun. The stories of Noah may happen appx. 5000 years ago in Turkey or Australia and that time there was no technology cars or airplane they rains few days they thought all world flooded they riding with donkey , no man can build a ship with wood they can hold 2 elephants and 2 donkey few monkey or cows.

RELIGIOUS LAWS

• Those teaching of powerful leaders such as Moses, Jesus and Mohamad, have been used as a way of to make a laws and manager to lead the people poor or rich many years to present times.
• There came a time when the traditional king and ministers couldn't do all of the laws in society and time passes and rise of army and dictator like Alexander the great or Genghis khan the balance of power eventually shifted from wisdom and experience, traditional modes of management and laws techniques to army and relied on ruthless and muscle or physical powers destroyed these may wisdoms or modes.

RELIGION SAMBAL

MEDIEVAL PERIOD LAWS

• Financial control and record keeping in the form of writing on clay tablets as well as on the stone walls in pyramids and buildings was seen during this time period. In ancient times management was not verbalized until Socrates and Plato. Chines philosophers had recognized the need of laws too. The Greeks provide documentation of universal view of management and laws. In the Medieval period when the Roman Empire fell the people of western Europe were reduced to basic needs of self-preservation and connected jiggle puzzle of name and numbers to new way of management and laws to follow the evil period all the way to todays to eventually end of the world with human activity and unknowing human past to destroy him or herself as name of religious or MAs ayah or Jesus or Mohamad come back again which is most comes from medieval period.

FEUDALISM PERIOD

- Roman landowner was somewhat feudalistic with the king or Caesar settling disputes between larger and wealthier landlord and smaller or poorer ones the latter being forced to give up the land holdings in exchange for protection from all out occupation by the more feudalistic thoughts and laws. There were no written laws or managerial concepts during this time.
- Feudalism did teach some laws and managerial premises that of controlling the means of production. The wealthy looking to maximize the richness of the land the owned pushed to reap from the poor during the dark ages.

FEUDALISM PERIOD LAWS

- During the dark ages people lived under great stress and strain. Feudalism prevailed and races of people were enslaved by others of their own race for being within the lower class in societies.
- These early managerial and laws to practiced was reflected of the dark side of humanity.

RENAISSANCE

- New ideas about laws organization and managing during medieval times awoke to Renaissance in England during the late sixteen to eighteen century. Everything was changed dramatically known as the industrial revolution. A new approach to laws and management developed as radical changes in production of tangible goods through invention, resulted in the factory system. The innovation itself was new goods affected both the means and processes of production and laws as well as domestic life in general and new laws.

RENAISSANCE

INDUSTRIAL REVOLUTION

- The industrial revolution was a time of unprecedented laws and improvements of manufacturing, management and law making reflecting these improvements.
- Structures changing to laws in nineteenth century were scientific laws with sociology and psychology of human being with behaviors changes.

EIGHTEEN AND NINETEEN CENTURY
LAWS

- The eighteen and nineteenth century marked the beginning of scientific laws with discovery of U.S.A and writing the united states constitution on new country and freedom of writing and speech and having arm or gun change the worlds of laws and regulation. New laws were almost importance to development of laws and management. Significant influence law maker and politician like George Washington or Abraham Lincoln in U.S.A and Gandhi in India, Lenin in Russia wrote on the science of laws and psychology for human behaviors and how leadership lead us to today's laws and management in twentieth century.

FUTURE OF LAWS AND MANAGEMENT

- How does one develop a vision of future of the laws and human behaviors? Some new leaders with a mission to change are naturally inclined toward speculating on what the leader would be like if he or she was ideal. Some leaders tend to take things as they are and do the best they can. Other leaders can quickly consider requirement of some structural model. How some leaders choose to craft a personal experience to correlated between their preferences of law and enforcement toward the employees or people.

FUTURE OF LAWS

- Law makers who rely on pull mechanisms picture groups of people who are energized and exited are future of the laws. Some leader in future and presents have personal vision is also affected by personal social drives in lawmaking. Those with high needs for achievement usually envision competitive, fast paced environment that meet challenging objectives. Those with a strong need for affiliation with mental pictures see people working closely together to attain shared organizational goals or nation laws with world peace, those who seek a sense of control and influences over others may have a picture of future lawmaking.

VISION OF THE LAWS

- Vision of future of the laws are process of creating an opinion of experience and learning of technology and history with having right tools and good foundation for culture and psychology. we most know the time is view of mental picture of reaction of problem and solving those problems with clear mind for lawmaking.
- Vision is writing the law with problem solving also have all tools of communication with simplified of all learning process is future of lawmaking for all humans.

HUMAN SENSES

- The future is already happening today. It is difficult to try and predict the future of laws, but it is good that we try to prepare for it. My theory of human has 9 senses is so powerful that it can change every phase of science, behaviors and laws, as well as people. The subject matter of my theory comes from my experience and search of myself and understanding of my anatomy and dealing with others. Usually we learn human has 5 senses 10 thousand years same mistakes. Human have several holes in his or her body which all related to senses of human senses of seeing, hearing, smelling, testing, touching and senses of sexuality and sense of relief and, we have senses of speaking. And last sense is sense of telepathy or in religion sense of soul.

SENSES

- We are in new millennium we need new revolutionary ideas on any topics. I choose human senses which I discovered human has 9 senses. This idea which will last for many generations I believed it and it will change the past psychology we need it to discuss, researches changing. We learn how we can change some laws; we learn how to love and how to hate how we act with each other's and how to know our self. What we have learned what is true and what is false or valid or invalid is the question of the past. I ask again is the color of one's skin or language one we speak or one religion or gender we have all can be solved with human senses. I ask again to do we know ourselves to judge others and make a laws.

play later here today so please ozone levels so please keep this in mind for the afternoon any sort of respiratory ailments even asthma can be impacted so remain indoors and try and help out others don't gas up your car do what you can just to keep the atmosphere as clean as possible

9 SENSES

- For generation to generation we learned wrong things. The information has been taught by schools and parents was wrong. For example, the humans have only five senses which all hole we have in body related to human senses and human has 9 senses.
- The nose is used for smelling and sense of smell, which is holes in nose.
- The ears are used for listening and sense of hearing and 2 holes each side of head.
- The eyes and used to see sense of vision and two holes of eyes in face.

9 SENSES

- The tongue or mount is used to tested different foods and sense of taste.
- There is also the sense of touch
- However, there are more holes in bodies human being can making sounds or noise human can speak we hear with ears we can speak with voice box in mount ability to make sound is other sense of human. Of course, some people speak very well and some not like politician and this sense is stronger than others. Speaking is a sense which is one of tools of communication and like the other senses people can learned vocabulary words and pronunciations language this a learning process and is shaped by life experiences.

9 SENSES

- The human body have several openings or holes which one opening is in the front of the body penis for male and vagina for female. And we can call it sense of sexuality.
- The other hole is at the back of human body anus with this opening we relief our self and provides an exit for digested food. When the stomach is full one feels uncomfortable going to bathroom and we call it sense of relief. Without this sense of relief with freedom being uncomfortably full it would be difficult to enjoy the pleasures of food.

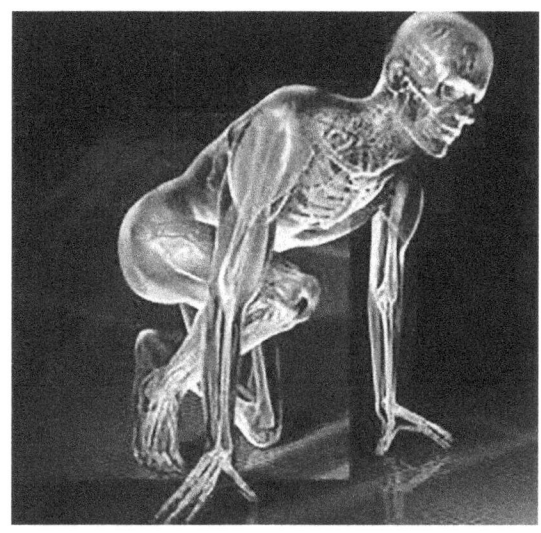

9 SENSES

•Sex in all societies remains a problem because from the beginning of the life to end it is not used in the right way. Lectures in schools and obligatory talks about the birds and bees, by parents, created misunderstanding due to the lack of knowledge and experience of young people as well as the wrong teaching.

•By studying these additional senses in human being psychology will change my theories of the study will revolutionize psychology laws. Philosophies, society. When children are taught to use all senses well, we have less problems in our society, Family are healthy Societies. we have healthy societies and less discrimination less crime, there won't be homosexual, praetor, or other bad behaviors in societies.

SENSES

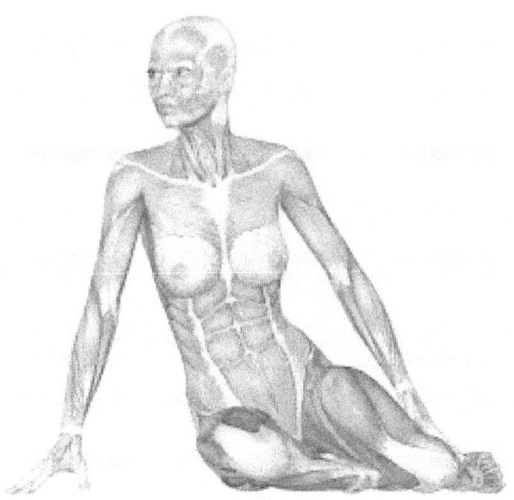

9 SENSES

• Finally. The combination of all impulses from all senses travels to brain creating the last sense. Sense of telepathy or in religion we call it sense of soul, we can love, or we can hate. I believe the human brain has low electricity and radio wave human like radio or cordless cell phone transmitted and received for communication. Unfortunately, still there is no device to measure human brain wave and I hope some days soon we can invent this devise that we can talk to each other's on silent with imagination of having company.

SENSES AND LAWS

- It is important that with good learning process of all senses we see world around us more accurately. If as a lawmaker, we see the people with all aspects of senses we can provide better problem solving.
- if someone we see discriminate because of lack of one senses or few senses we understand all humans are not perfect and we write the laws to balance those human weaknesses.

LIFESPAN BASE ON 9 SENSES

- Lifespan base on 9 senses,
- cultural differences, and stereotype in psychology:
- By:
- Majid Khodabandeh

9 SENSES

- Introduction:
- The theory of humans has 9 senses is my idea since 1993 which I wrote in one of my undergraduate classes in Norther Kentucky University long time ago. I am proud I published the book, legal concept of law and human behavior senses. (2009). Amazon.com To protect my Idea about this important concept.
- Still after 23 years passing, if I am in class of psychology, or with friends and relatives no one knows what I am trying to say or what I am talking about this new discovery. Still is a new subject human have 9 senses vs. we learned human has only 6 senses. I am taking in it very seriously and I believe past information was not perfect. I feel I have obligation to this important message, and I want to send my message throw my books to everyone understand human have nine senses in the world.

HOLES IN BODY

- Introduction:
- Basically, any hole in body human have, are relation to human senses. Very basic understandings of human being are understanding of human anatomy and what a perfect human is. Human senses are, Sense of seeing or visions are 2 holes of eyes. Senses of hearing are 2 holes of ears in head. Senses of smell are 2 holes in nose in face. Sense of test or hole of mount in face with the tong, there are 2 more holes in humans' bodies holes in front of the men or women which is sense of sexuality, and hole in back which is sense of relief which I add this 2 senses, to old senses. Of course, we can add 2 old senses which are senses of touch and senses of telepathy are senses too and I am not against those senses. There is one more sense still, and is Sense of speaking and ability human can speak with tools of mount,
- tong and voice box, which is 3rd senses I add to old senses.
- Human can speak we can hear with ears and they can respond with speaking sense which if we hear we don't respond we have very bad feeling and human ability to speak is other sense of human also make a perfect human. Total all these senses are making it human being have nine senses. I am trying in this book clear Lifespan of human being with having all senses from early child hood to late adulthood , how to satisfy all senses from childhood to all the way adulthood to enjoy the life understanding laws and concepts to find a solution to problems with a peace and healthy body and mind also healthy societies . How to be a perfect human being with less psychological problems less crime in society less problems in family and friendship is a goal of understanding of all senses.
- These explanations will also change some Laws and we wrote better Laws in community and nation or in the world to live with peace and understanding of humans needs.

EARLY CHILDHOOD

- Presenting Challenges for early childhood:
- What is solution for early childhood psychology is question of these researches? What can mother or father doing to teach right things to our children, how society must act, how government and taxpayer must response to such a situation. All are questions in this book. Such a powerful country like U.S.A with strong economic must have always to take care of children and lead the world everybody can follow. I will mention all needs of children is in general same into society and always we can solve problems to know the needs and satisfaction of senses. We as a psychologist must be finding a right solution for children of the world and how to keep healthy society are goals in General Psychology. To solve those very common issues like health care in society with study of economic, finance, environmental, science, technology, culture, values, psychology, etc. I ask myself how American with such a strong economy should have free education, free healthcare and solve lots of psychological problems in society.

DATA BASES

- I will use researches to conduct my scholarly databases for early childhood development. To learn educational Psychology need it a lot of effort with critical thinking, about human Senses. Human senses are the key for childhood development. With good training, good communication tools for kids we can succeed educational psychology during lifespan. To choose my topic and analyzing of strength and weaknesses I am very confident of the Theory of human has nine senses in general psychology, we have an impact to our children. Good vision of new idea can solve today's psychology problems. To lead knowledge of psychology for future early childhood development we need good foundation of human beings with the vision of human has nine senses.

POSSIBLE THEORY

- Identification of Possible Theory-or Research- Based Alternatives:
- In the past psychology some psychologist talking about Eight Stage of life span which Erikson's, said, he said in first stage of lifespan in early childhood, is trust versus mistrust, which is for children between, births to 2 years old. I am not agreeing with Erikson in this idea. I think children still didn't learned trust or mistrust in early age and it is not making senses trust or mistrust in this stage, it is nature of human being. Baby has no other choices and human baby 100% need help to survive. In this case any kid's may unable to do any things just mistrust everybody in class and her behavior is cause bad reaction, because he or she didn't eat well or sleeping well. In some cases, early stage of lifespan for human babies, like 6 months babies have understanding less than monkey babies in the same age. Human baby in the same age in early stages of childhood development are not smarter than monkeys in 6 months old. For example, of ball under the hat which human baby don't understand where ball is but baby monkey knows where ball is.
- Vygotsky's sociocultural theory (2012). of development in environment it is describe very effectively in this case study, and influence of any kid's in family with society. kid's interactions with other kids influence her cognitive understanding or misunderstanding of the others and he or she was upset and throwing toys to other kids are the question of lack of sleep or less food. kid's or children with different culture or race or gender can be describing in this case is not true statement of problems, and roots of problems are not having good food or good sleep in most cases.
- Study of kid's has a bioecological theory too,(e.g., Brenden
Brenner & Ceci,
1994). Can be discuss with her parent and Bio- social ecological theory which how Kid's lifespan develops with some socio-cultural theories and found the solution for her problem

IMPACT OF INDIVIDUAL

1. Impact of individual and Cultural differences on lifespan development
2. To understand cultural in early childhood Vygotsky's said sociocultural theory (e.g., 1934, 1978). He has a view of development of Child's lifespan. How culture can influence social interactions like language or color of one's skin, or one's religion or gender, all can be problems in todays of world of children. Finding solution with analysis of childhood development is always question. Good educational system can solve discrimination caused by these differences in early

childhood development. Lack of one understands of oneself can be misunderstanding our body from childhood to adulthood can cause problems for good values and good cultural differences? I asked again, do we know ourselves well enough to treat children or others as a psychologist? Or like the other wrong doctors prescribe pain killer that will brings bigger problems for individual or family. For generations, wrong information has been taught by both schools and parents alike. For example, the human being has five senses.

HUMAN HOLES IN BODY

Which are nine senses actually? Human have hole in the body related to human senses, like eyes or ears or nose, or mounts, others holes in body that are sense like hole in front (vagina, penis) of body or sense of sexuality and hole in back (anuses) , sense of relief, sense of speaking, sense of soul or telepathy, which human has total nine senses. Society remains have problems, because from the beginning of the life to the end it is not used in the right way. Lectures in schools and obligatory talks about the birds and bees, by parents, create misunderstanding due to the lack of knowledge and experience of young people, as well as the archaic analogies used in teaching. By studying these additional senses in human psychology, all the present theories and study of behavior can be changed; thus, revolutionizing the laws in general psychology which, how human being in society. When our children are taught to use these additional senses properly, society and family will be healthier. There will be less discrimination and less crime less psychological issues with good education.

EVIDENCE OF 9 SENSES

- Evidence- based Theory Support for Interventions:
- The value of this Idea of Human has 9 senses will "In cognitive psychology the term problem solving refers to the mental process that people go through to discovery of themselves and analyze to solving problems. This involves all the steps in the problem process, including the discovery of the problem, the decisions to tackle the issue, understanding the problem, researching the available options and taking actions to achieve the goals. Which describe in" Stemberg, R.(2003). Cognitive psychology.
Belmont, CA: Wadsworth.

CHILDHOOD AND 9 SENSES

- What is childhood development conclusion in psychology base on 9 senses:
- Kid's problems understand of general psychology for all parents and teachers, which cause by lack of foods or sleeps. Educational learning is process of human being in different stages of lifespan. Understanding of all humans' basic needs are most important issues, to have healthy children. Presenting this case study problem is to analyze all aspects of this case study with new vision of human body and human has nine senses is most important to analysis for that case study for childhood development. I did analysis, who is perfect human being. To inform kid's mother and father, are sometimes aggressive behaviors in preschool we need to see all the basic Dawn's needs satisfy. If our children in any case study like, Ali's, Syma's, Dawn's Mike's, Sam's or others satisfied his or her needs in propitiate matter problem will be solved. In any kid's case study we was trying to answer relationship between children behavior in preschool and home with strategic plan solving educational system about behaviors with human senses and satisfaction of all senses and needs. In general psychology to analysis strengths and weakness of that research are good idea of human have 9 senses are satisfaction of all senses.

9 SENSES

- It is important, and it is the key of success we know foundation of human being is human have nine senses. I am confident if our kids have enough foods and sleeps, lots of problems will solves. I can admit in most cases teachers and parents have fewer problems with kids. When we satisfy all needs, we have fewer problems. Parents and teachers with disciplinary action can teach to our children, human has nine senses; it will be solving lots of problems in childhood development. Lifespan also in any stages of life must be based on this foundation, which human have 9 senses.

CHILDHOOD AND SENSES

•Introduction to middle childhood lifespan base on 9 senses:
•No doubt about it, to give teenagers peer review everyday it is most important lesson of lifespan for middle age childhood development. Parents or teachers can simply give good advice every day with respect and teaching new skills to middle childhood kids. Teaching right things to teenager is the key success for our children also learning with respect. We must try to avoid too much humors and more lesson to teach in teenagers with more respects. Good attitude from parents with respectable behaviors, with good communication skills, and use of right tools like internet, media, good videos all can be build a world of youth population in right manners. To understand environments parents, or society, neighbors, and friend's middle childhood is process of better understanding.

RESEARCHES

• According to today's researches, right now close to two billion of population of the world are middle age children. My focus of this book is to analysis all Cases studies of general psychology for middle childhood development. To take look at the immigrant kids and family who are living in united State from different countries is the focus of this book too. How Lifespan in his middle children can change his, or her image and how teenager's family or any immigrants affects different stage of lifespan different from origin countries. This teenager case study is analysis of problems for most teenagers with family, which they have teenagers' children around 12 years old, to 18 years old are my focus on those teenagers especially if they are immigrant, which have different languages from English. Difficulty about language is very problematic for immigrants, Mexican,
German, Asian European, African all have problems, when coming to U.S. for pronunciation the words or memorizing the words are very difficult and time consuming. To understanding the words, they must look for definition and look like it is impossible to get the perfect grades. Possibility of bulling and make a fun with depression and loneliness are cause problem for those middle age children. I understand this issue very well and I had same problem when I came to U.S.A , Instead of this case study kids was 16 and 17 years old, I was 29 years old when I was arrival to U.S .

DIFFICULTY

•I had lots of difficulty to speak the English language and still after 26 years I have my own accent and lack of vocabulary, which I suppose to learned it in my early childhood or in middle childhood and I don't have those words or vocabulary with a right pronunciation which still make it very difficult for me to express myself.

PRIMARY ISSUES

•Primary Issues:
•To look at the Lifespans in middle childhood development are to understand of middle childhood development. Teenagers around 16 years old middle age children are usually as a typically sophomore, high school students. They are living with family rich or poor, educated or uneducated black or white, Asian or Hispanic, Arabs, or Hindu, all, are young humans trying to pass the stages of life. Some are shy, some are with values or deep cultures, some with different languages or different religion or background, some interested of sport or music's or arts, some

GROUP AGES

• interested on science and math or history. All those group ages are concerning of the world of education and discovery of themselves and all surrounding. Some with poor grades in school and some with good grades, some blaming on the others like teacher, or parents are caused to falls for bad performance or good grades. Some saying education or learning experience was boring and not interested anymore and going for drugs or alcohol, smoking, or playing games or gambling. They may ask for driving the car or go to friend's house which those behaviors is not acceptable in some families or schools. Some of them get bad grades and felling during school times. Some kids they have too much freedom from parents some too much control. Teenagers are usually making mistakes for decision making because of lack of experience. Also, some teenagers may start to have drinking underage, or smoke or other problems like bully or sex in teenager time. But I am saying all must have same common and all human have nine senses which we must focus on this important and change the direction to this important point of psychology.

HUMAN HAS 9 SENSES

•Presenting Challenges base on human have 9 senses:
•What is the solution for all teenagers? What are the challenges? What can mother, and father doing, to prevent them for faller, how society and friends must do to clear all challenges. How government and taxpayer must response in such a situation, all are my questions and my challenges. What we as a psychologist must do to found out a right solution for middle age children of the world. How we can keep healthy society with General Psychology. Education psychology understands of any stage of life. We must, especially prevent the alcohol, or drugs, smoking in middle age and take them under control with right educational learning progress which is another big challenge.

THEORY OF HUMAN BEING

•Identification of Possible Theory- or Research- Based Alternatives
•(Siegel & scovill, 2000, P. 781) said; "while problem behaviors was largely socialized" through the 1960's, it has become "medicalized" in the 1990. In an age in which we have been led to believe that there is a "magic scientific bullet" for nearly all physiological and social problems, we have medicalized" and behaviors problems are "there's nothing we could do; our child was born a delinquent."
•There was breaking news in T.V yesterday, they were saying teenage after injury if he or she go the doctor, doctor prescribe the teenagers pain killer which end up the use of heroin and bad drugs which doctors must be very careful to prescribe pain killer for teenagers and put some kid's in trouble . Laws must protect all children; doctors can't prescribe pain killer anymore and there was saying every 33 minutes someone ding from drug overdose which is even more than car accident deaths in U.S.A.

TEENAGERS AND SENSES

•To solve those very common issues for teenagers like socialization, drugs or alcohol, smoking and sex we must educated our children toward healthy and right education. To analyze lifespan in this group ages we must study different theories and study of lifespan in the right way and ignore all wrong past information, which I think all theories like Erikson, Fraud's, Padgett's are in some stand wrong for today's children. We must teach and practice good behaviors which Erikson's, or Fraud's said some of the stages of lifespan are wrong images. We must clear the road for new generation and realize impacts of economic, environmental, science, technology, culture, values, are important with good practice of psychology. Psychologist and Politician must have strategic plan to have free education, free healthcare, international agricultures, cheap shelter, food, transportation with new technology to achieve all needs of family to solving lots of psychological problems in world.

9 SENSES

•Lifespan must be focus on middle age children about additional senses newly discover for human being. To understanding of middle childhood, we must learn human has nine senses. How human senses can impact of all stages of lifespan, how this discovery of human has nine senses will help childhood lifespan to develop. It is important with additional senses of human, like Senses of sexuality, sense of relief, sense of speech, sense of telepathy, most problems in middle childhood will be solved. To start the development those additional three senses in this part of the lifespan can keep the teenager busy with himself or herself for solo playing. If teenager to stay in his, or her room and watching video and pictures and reading interesting books to pass this stage of life more easily pass throw lifespan. Self-study of teenagers will describe those senses with storytelling or science telling, they will stop madness in this stage of life for adolescent and youth.

9 SENSES

•To repeat the Idea of human has nine senses and additional 3 more senses to all middle childhood lifespan in the world are to use cog book, which presents a new way of learning. Aim is to change General Psychology based on the idea that a human has nine senses and less discus about the Erikson's theory or Fraud's Idea or Piaget's stages in middle childhood. The discovery of humans having nine senses will open the door for humankind. Focus of this paper is to use researches to conduct my scholarly databases for early childhood, and middle age development, for Educational Psychology, also for Elementary schools, high schools, and all critical thinking, of Human being in general psychology. How we can teach the children to Communication, and solving problems, especially in teenagers ages. Educational psychology is complex, and it will begin for learning experience during lifespan. In General psychology foundation base will be on human senses. To have a good vision of new idea, which today's psychology can lead knowledge of future childhood development. The theory of human has nine senses will be revolutionary Idea in childhood development psychology and will change the lifespan during any stage of development. To understanding of human anatomy and relation to any hole in body we have, to clarify all humans have those same holes we can see and feel in all nine senses of human being, which is perfect human being and childhood development develop.

VALUES

•Impact of individual Cultural differences in middle childhood development:
•To understand values and cultural in middle childhood problems in today's world like foreigner teenagers with different culture or languages in different country is not acceptable for global world and new educational system. Problems can be solved by these differences. Lack of one understands of values of lifespan in middle childhood cause misunderstanding of parents or teachers and lack of development of educational system. For generations, wrong information has been taught by both schools and parents alike. For example, the human being has five senses. Which was the nose is used for smelling- sense of smell. The ears are used for listening- sense of hearing. The eyes are used to see – sense of vision. The tongue is used to tested different foods- sense of taste. Touch senses and feeling. Human have more senses. There is also other holes in body that are sense like hole in front of body or sense of sexuality and hole in back, sense of relief, sense of speaking, sense of soul or telepathy, which human has total nine senses.

SENSES

•The human being can make noise and can speak by making sounds using voice box located at the base of the throat; therefore, the voice the ability to make sound is another sense of human. Of course, some people speak very well, or see better than others. Some people use one sense more than other senses, for example, musicians use listening skills a lot, and writers use their eyes extensively. Speaking is a sense which is one the main form of communication, like the other senses people learn and have memory enabling them to recall faces, and vocabulary words and their pronunciations- language, this learning process is shaped by life experiences. The human body has several openings or holes, all these holes are related to sense, organs like nose, eyes, ears, and mouths, all are instruments for our senses. There are two more holes in the body; one is at the front of our body- penis for male, and Vagina for female. The other hole is at the back of the body- anus. The hole is front called sense of sex. With this hole, one can feel the pleasures of having sexual intercourse. Fraud Idea was about only affect all children lifespan about the sex and human behaviors was only around a sex and love of mother or father which are not right.

DISCOVERY OF HUMAN SENSES

•The other discovery of senses is the anise- the hole in the back, which is the sense in that, provides an exit for digested food and it is one of the most part of the human sense. When the stomach is full and one feels uncomfortable, going to the bathroom provides a feeling of relief and sense of relief. Without this sense of relief human being are uncomfortably full, it would be difficult to enjoy and having pleasures of food.
•Sex, Drugs, Alcohol, in all society remains a problem, from the beginning of the life especially in middle childhood lifespan it is issue of lifespan like in , teenager like Mark's, Dean's, Hyun, Ki's , Ali's, Jose's , Joe's, Paul's, John's, Mohamad's, Magen's, Sally's, Max's, Nora's, Majid's Mina's cases. Sex knowledge is not used in the right way with

good values and human understanding in today society. Again, Lectures in schools and obligatory talks about the birds

PAST IDEA

- and bees, by parents, create misunderstanding due to the lack of knowledge and experience of young people, as well as the archaic analogies used in teaching. By studying these additional senses in human psychology, all the present theories and study of behavior can be changed; thus, revolutionizing the laws, general psychology in human being in society. When our children are taught to use these additional senses properly, society will be healthier. There will be less discrimination and less crime. There won't be homosexuality nor sicknesses associated with bad sexual behavior.
- Also, there is other sense which is the combination of the impulses from all senses travels to brain creating the last sense, or telepathy, in religion this sense called soul. We love and we hate, and religion thinks it is connection to God or gospel and holy spirts.

SENSE OF 9TH

- I believe the human brain functions like radio or cordless computer or phone containing short waves that can be transmitted and received for communication. Unfortunately, still there is no device to measure this sense, and I hope someday we can invent this important devise that we can talk to each other on silent and we don't need cell phone.
- The value of this Idea of Human has 9 senses will be revolutionizing the psychology problem- solving for middle age childhood to the mental issues and process that people go through to discover and solving problems. To write a clear problem statement in my topic, which is the general psychology on Educational, my assignment requires to critical thinking of what are my solution on my topic in case study of problem solving for middle childhood development . To State the research problem solving for teenagers' problems, I needed to summarize what human anatomy are?, what human know so far and what is my new idea of my knowledge about my topic which is middle childhood development with additional senses in human being.
- Additional senses we must teach it to middle childhood development are.

SENSE OF SEXUALITY

- Sense of sex:
- This sense is growing understanding from early childhood to middle childhood and early adulthood must be more research about this important issue. For example, what are we must start to teach this additional sense to boys and girls. Also, human sense of sex is not related to faith or sin what we learned in past. It is most important things we must teach separation of human being in religion and what real lifespan are without any bad teaching of Devil, or Sin, or seitan which is not exist. It is important to understand with imagination things in sense of soul bring the love in lifespan. We must teach it right to everybody to prevent our kids from bad things like suicide in teenager time is miss understanding of sin or faith with religion can cause bad behaviors. When sense of sex is not clear understanding what are love or joules needs of humans ignore can cause problems. We must make sure it is the anatomy and understanding of human being and this organs of human is only one of 9 senses of human which we must balance the life with all of senses not just focus on one sense which Freud's idea was only to focus on sex was wrong.

SENSE OF RELIEF

- Sense of relief:
- This sense is like the other senses from early age kids will learn how to control, how to enjoy foods, and when they can relief of digested foods. Basic knowledge of this sense can direct the humans and all our children to right direction. Of course use of this sense is a way to not to go in the wrong direction in sex activities and possibility of sicknesses and dirty condition and sickness of dirty hole, desists like Aids or other sickness which they must teach with good educational system to all humankind.

SENSE OF SPEAKING

- Sense of speaking:
- Without communication human being can't say his or her needs and this sense it is one of the most important senses that can brings the human being in very high level of career today. Hyun- Ki's family can speak 2 languages which it is in some point winner. But living in U.S and not perfectly speak English language is the weakness in any job or schools. It might cause low self-steams or psychological problem for family. I think If we can teach to our kids, how to speaks properly, how to explain things well, how explain his or her needs, how to sings or how-to defendant her or his self from very early age it is the key to success. This speaking sense is a life saver and it is most important sense to have good careers and today's problem solving. I believe world must learned to speaking only one sense and politician use only this sense to improve the situation which is not good aspect of see the human or people and judge just what they are saying. I also want to introduce my book of world language which I said all humans must learned to speak only one language in future to have sense of understanding and no conflicts or miss understanding or discrimination based on languages.

SENSE OF LOVE OR HATE

- Sense of soul, telepathy, love, or hate:
- After we teach to the kids all senses which we must teach them in all stage of lifespan, we must
Understanding of combination of all senses travels to brain and humans have a feeling of love or hate. Of course all senses was agreeing or disagree, like or dislike or like can be loves or hate , what was learned as a good values about different religions or faith they will build a foundation of behaviors of peace , good cultural and good values, which will effect children and adult's lifespan . Good behaviors for decision making and passing the good lifespan are the balance of all senses are sense of soul, or telepathy.

MIDDLE CHILDHOOD

- Evidence- based Theory support for interventions.
- To analysis all evidence of all ages especially middle childhood development is understanding of human have 9 senses, which we were learned in past was not perfect human being. This idea human has nine senses will change direction of lifespan. What we have learned in past was wrong? What is true, and what is not true, in childhood development, to adulthood are evidence. How we can educate middle childhood kids to plays the role of middle childhood development.
- According to Piaget's and Erikson's, Fraud theories, all lifespan Stages of mankind development are not perfect analyses. Concrete operational stage" (Broderick & Blewitt, P. 2015. P.205), it is not any more Concrete education, which they saying in middle childhood, are stage of Isolation young adulthood is wrong, or Identity versus role of confusion is wrong and children must have no confusion the way we teach them lesson, or stage of values and vocational goals which can be for every individual different with different environment in lifespan. All past theories can't be explored in wrong direction for analyses in middle age of childhood development. Base on my theory of human have 9 senses. That means all old theories like Piaget's and Erikson's eight stages of lifespan or Fraud's sexuality theory are not true for today childhood, middle childhood or adulthood development.

MIDDLE CHILDHOOD

- What are the Conclusion for middle childhood development?
- In today society's problems in middle childhood behaviors are challenging. To know human has 9 senses and satisfy all human senses during all stages of lifespan, is understanding of structure educational learning on any acts of psychology. To analysis all research around this general educational psychology, we must solve problems and providing more work for this research. To achieve a goal and to write this assignment for middle childhood development my focus was aim on those studies. To analysis all answer with all solution for all Middle childhood development need more work done. To understanding of human anatomy relation with environment, with cultural differences attitude, language differences, races genders differences, and how learning experiences can be teaching kid's with strategic plan solving problems. We need more time to research. Focus of this book is to teach educational learning for middle childhood behaviors. How to teach our kid's or all humans in different stage of life, how we can with all senses in lifespans development and how to

satisfy all needs of human in any stages of life with all senses is most important aspects of this research. Analysis strengths and weakness of this research for middle childhood was discovery of human have 9 senses. We still needed to work hard for more researches to be done. I am confident we can teach to children, parents and teachers with disciplinary action human have nine senses, and how we can solve lots of problems

9 SENSES

•In middle childhood or other stages of lifespans in life. I am looking forward to writing more in psychology about human have nine senses.
•This Summary also answers some solution for all middle children like,
Mohamed or Ali, or Sun, or Hyun Ki's, John, Jose, Joe, Paul, Sarah's Dawn's, Mohammad's and so on family. Understanding of human anatomy relation with environment, with cultural differences, language differences, race and gender differences, how we can with strategic plan solving problems for educational system. How we can see perfect behaviors and, how to be learning human senses in middle childhood lifespan is important job to parents and schoolteachers. To analysis strengths and weakness of my research we must have idea which makes a perfect sense. I think human have 9 senses vs. of 6 senses. My focuses of this paper were for middle childhood development. I am confident if my goal is to teach parents and teachers with disciplinary action human senses, it will solve lots of problems in lifespan especially for middle childhood development. To understand and solving the problems like, Dean, Hyun-Ki's, Angela's and Adam's, Dawn's, Mark's, Sarah's, and so on case in society or family we need to understanding, human have nine senses vs. six senses we learned, which will be foundation of future psychology.

ADULTHOOD

•Introduction of Adulthood:
•To look at adulthood Lifespan is understanding of ages between 20 to 60 years old, white or black or others races as a typical adult which are working as a labors or human resource supervisor doctor, engineers, etc. and all are working in different companies , married men, or married women, married twice or several times. He, or she have children, and his, or her ex-wife or husband they have step kids goes to school or college who has financial difficulty for his tuition are most problems of adulthood. If second marriage is with other who have the kids, are more challenging. For past several years be a mother or father to help the kids who are need more help and those marriage more problematics.

PROBLEMS

•Primary issues and Presenting Problems:
•What is the solution for adult's problems? What are the cultural, values, financial problems? How adulthood can be healthy. How he, or she can solve his problems. How society and friends must do to help adult ages, how family can have influences on this relationship and how he can have healthy body and mind. What we as a psychologist must do to find a right solution for adulthood in the world and how we can keep healthy family and society with General Psychology Education.

SOLVING PROBLEMS

• To solve those very common issues for adulthood and, health issues in society we must study of human being in today's world. We must teach and practice who is perfect human being. How we can with stablish economic, finance, environmental, science, technology, culture, values, and good psychology, etc. How we can succeed in all stages of lifespan. I'll ask myself how we can as American lead the world with good values of human being, and how we can lead whole world to following us. How with strong economy we can as American face different issues for adulthood.
Psychologist and Politician can strategically plan to have free education, free healthcare, free club or gyms, more freedom for sex activity and writing and speech to solving lots of psychological problems.

SOLVING PROBLEMS

- Stemberg, R (2003) said there are a lot of different mental process at any job during solving- problems. "
- 1-Perceptually recognizing a problem.
- 2-Representing the problem in memory.
- 3- Considering relevant information that applies to the current problem.
- 4-Identify different aspects of the problem.
- 5-Labeling and describing the problem. "
- After traveling and living in Europe and Asia I realize Human lifespan was lots of challenging. I did understand in U.S.A and there is not too much freedom for sex and people are more religious' and conservatives.

LIFESPAN COMPLEXES

- I believe lifespan must be focus on this stage of lifespan which is adulthood about my idea of additional senses. As I said discovery of human has nine senses revolutionized the psychology and behaviors. Those additional senses, like Senses of sexuality, sense of relief, sense of speech, sense of telepathy all started to develop in all phase of lifespan especially in adulthood. We must teach those additional four senses in this part of the life span extensively. Adler's Psychologist said "humans' improvement in life have two motivation" 1st of all human has complexes like poor verses rich, not having the things to buy toys for kids or person whom

9 SENSES

- pursuing to have more money and don't have it and those complex cause to improve in life, and lack of sex and not having cute wife or husband or right partner or not having wife, or girlfriend or husband and those complexes cause to improve to better life . Today's society we have we can call it success or faller which we may be wrong in definition of success or faller which are all complex and it is not loss or gain just a sickness of not having things or not satisfying the senses.
- To keep the teenager, or early adulthood we must strategic plan for all stages life to make an adult or teenager busy with herself or himself for solo playing and to stay in his room and watching video and pictures and reading interesting books are the way to break the wall of complexes and it is understanding of themselves. Lack of sex or jealousy is discovering by just enjoy by him or herself for adult men or women buying sex without commitment is other way of reach this goal. Marriage sometimes is not fast solution, good experience which healthy society must have more freedom for sex for men and women. Healthy society understands sex and marriage or relationship in lifespan is very important. Self-study of human being which is describes nine senses are important. Storytelling or science telling, they will stop madness in teenager, or adult in some point. Most marriages not lass more than 4 years in today societies because there are a lot of desperate housewife or desperate house husband which if there was no jealousy and freedom for sex relationship and friendship last longer, and sense of sexuality only one sense of human.

9 SENSES

- I am going to repeat my Idea of human have nine senses to all human being in the world one more time again , which I think solve most of childhood, middle childhood and adulthood like Dave's or Sandy's, Ali's, Majid's, Mark's, Kim's, and so on behaviors in general psychology.
- Lifespan course uses the cog book, which is presents a new way of learning and I recommended this way of learning like Cog book for teenagers and adult. My aim is to use this way of learning for changing General Psychology based on the idea that human has nine senses. The discovery of humans having nine senses will open the door for humankind. I did focus to use for my researches to conduct my scholarly databases for early childhood, middle age development, and adulthood. Educational Psychology, in Elementary schools, high school, and college are educational learning, with critical thinking of human being and human has nine senses. Training with good communication skills to all kids and teenagers and adult is the key of success. Educational psychology is complex, and it will begin for learning experience during lifespan, which I can share my 57 years of experience to new theory of lifespan

9 SENSES

• To choose my topic and analyzing of strength and weaknesses I am very confident of the Theory of human has nine senses will change the psychology. General psychology will be new foundation is based on human has nine senses and vision of new idea, which today's psychology can lead knowledge of future all phase of lifespan development. My specialty for my dissertation will be on Educational Psychology Learning on human Senses. My idea about human senses is so powerful that can change the psychology in all phases of psychology. I believe human has nine senses verses, six senses we used to learned. This theory will be revolutionary Idea in childhood development psychology and will change the lifespan during any stage of life. To understanding of human anatomy and relation to any holes in body we have, to clarify all humans have those same holes we can see and feel in all nine senses of human being. It is perfect human being in childhood development, to adulthood development.

LIFESPAN BASED ON 9 SENSES

•Analysis of lifespan will be starting with human has 9 senses. What we know about past and present in childhood, and adulthood development, are new direction of lifespan. What have we learned in past was wrong? What is true, and what is not true is important to development of childhood development, how can education play the role of early childhood development is focus of my goal in this book.
•Identification of possible theory- or research- based alternative.
•Piaget's and Erikson's, Freud's theories, all have lifespan Stages of Mankind, which they saying in lifespan, or adulthood feeling like love of mother or father which still can shows in some adulthood lifespan which is wrong and different complex like Electoral or Deepti complexes are wrong messages or stage of Isolation young adulthood , or Identity versus role of confusion, or stage of values and vocational goals etc. are wrong base of my theory of human have 9 senses, and in lifespan Erikson's said are all challenges for kids and I am not agree for all those theories and all having lack of understanding of human anatomy and real human being for lifespan.

9 SENSES

•Impact of Cultural differences on development base on human have 9 senses.
•To understand cultural, color of one's skin, or language one speaks, or one's religion or gender, all problems in today's world can be solve with analysis of childhood development to adulthood development. Good educational system can solve discrimination caused by these differences. Lack of one understands of oneself and body from childhood cause misunderstanding of human being with different cultural and values differences? Asked again, do we know ourselves well enough to treat our children or others as a psychologist? For generations, wrong information has been taught by both schools and parents alike. For example, the human being has five senses. Which was the nose is used for smelling- sense of smell. The ears are used for listening sense of hearing. The eyes are used to see –sense of vision. The tongue is used to tested different foods- sense of taste. Touch senses and feeling. Human have more senses. There is also other holes in body that are sense like hole in front of body or sense of sexuality and hole in back, sense of relief, sense of speaking, sense of soul or telepathy, which human has total nine senses. The human being can make noise and can speak by making sounds using voice box located at the base of the throat; therefore, the voice the ability to make sound is another sense of human. Of course, some people speak very well, or see better than others. Some people use one sense more than other senses, for example, musicians use listening skills a lot, and writers use their eyes extensively. Speaking is a sense which is one the main form of communication, like the other senses people learn and have memory enabling them to recall faces, and vocabulary words and their pronunciations- language, this learning process is shaped by life experiences. The human body has several openings or holes, all these holes are related to sense, organs like nose, eyes, ears, and mouths, all are instruments for our senses. There are two more holes in the body; one is at the front of our body- penis for male, and Vagina for female. The other hole is at the back of the body- anus. The hole is front called sense of sex.

9 SENSES

- With this hole, one can feel the pleasures of having sexual intercourse and Freud Idea was about only these senses affect all children, or adult behaviors which are not right, and I am dis agree with Freud idea. The anise- the hole in the back is the sense in that provides an exit for digested food. When the stomach is full and one feels uncomfortable, going to the bathroom provides a feeling of relief and sense of relief. Without this sense of relief human being are uncomfortably full, it would be difficult to enjoy and having pleasures of food.
- Sex in all society remains a problem, because from the beginning of the life to the end it is not used in the right way. Lectures in schools and obligatory talks about the birds and bees, by parents, create misunderstanding due to the lack of knowledge and experience of young people, as well as the archaic analogies used in teaching. By studying these additional senses in human psychology, all the present theories and study of behavior can be changed; thus, revolutionizing the laws, general psychology in human being in society. When our children are taught to use these additional senses properly, society will be healthier. There will be less discrimination and less crime. There won't be homosexuality nor sicknesses associated with bad sexual behavior.

9 SENSES

- Also, other sense is the combination of the impulses from all senses travels to brain creating the last sense, or telepathy, in religion this sense called soul. We love and we hate.
- I believe the human brain functions like radio or cordless computer or phone containing short waves that can be transmitted and received for communication. Unfortunately, still there is no device to measure this sense, and I hope someday we can invent this important devise that we can talk to each other on silent and we don't need cell phone.
- The value of this Idea of Human has 9 senses will" In cognitive psychology the term problem- solving refers to the mental process that people go through to discover, analyze and solve problems. Stemberg, R. (2003)." This involves all of the steps in the problem process, including the discovery of the problem, the decisions to tackle the issue, understanding the problem, researching the available options and taking actions to achieve my goals." Stemberg, R.(2003). Cognitive psychology. Belmont, CA: Wadsworth.

CULTURAL DIFFERENCES

- Interventions, impact of individual and cultural differences on development and stereotype:
- To addressing how different cultures formed with all complexities of race, religious, genders and wealth etc. in societies are research of history with a vision of the world, study of present with experience and knowledge of science and facts, also for future of new culture.
- To analyze stereotype with a direction of humanity, to all cultural are learning experience with vision of the right way of doing things or wrong way of doing things. All individuals or all countries are missing the point in case of culture to others and somehow everybody have attitude or behaviors problems, because any culture is not perfect. Part of my mission is to analyze and research study of stereotype counties which I saw during my lifespan as my research these issues. As I told you I traveled a lot and I used to live in Germany. I came to promos land United States after I lived in Europe. I meet a lot of different people with different nationalities and races, or genders, Gay, Lesbian, straight, you name it. I was always wondering things how was written in history of world as a stereotype. few years ago I had a Indian friends which he wants me to paint his deck and he invited me to his basement I saw in his wall there was a poster with broken cross in basement wall or "swastika" symbol of Nazi or Fascism

NATIONALISM

- I was scare at the first, who is this man. I went home Google under "religions symbol's" I saw is broken cross is symbol of one of the biggest religious in India and Hitler learned from these religion's and adopted that symbol for Nazi, which is Indian name. This symbol has a name "Nazi" which is a name of flower in Indian or in Asian language. Like shamrock leaf for St. Patrick's religious symbol and Nuns and Priest does not get married. Sham which is candle and rocks and sham rock in Asian language is "shab nam , which means "night is wet, and rocks, Please go deep to understanding this concept I said about stereotype. I also need it different study researches in these similarity stereotypes religious write too. However, I am realizing Indian culture or German how promote the Nationalism which is wrong culture for today's world.

• These nations teach to citizen how is a culture of nation, how to use own cloths or own food or own technology, married only with a same race or with only own culture, which is wrong for today's world. Hitler learned of these ideological concepts, all were, with own silence attitude and thinking of destroy other nations or cultures which is wrong, and these cultures are deep in roots of any nations.

• Back to painting the deck, also he paid me for more than 3000 sq ft deck 300.00$ which had more than 3000.00$ value of labors, I did for only 300 hundred. I think these are biggest stereotype of the world cultures and make a world miserable to other nations or religions which are all stereotypes world cultures with bad attitude. These thoughts can cause conflicts and psychological problems to individuals or countries.

EDUCATION ON GENERAL PSYCHOLOGY

• To write a clear problem statement in my topic, which is the general psychology on Educational, in my book requires to critical thinking of what are my solution on my topic are in case study of problem solving , I needed 3 significant thinking process. I must State the research problem solving for kids and adult. I needed to summarize what human anatomy are in any culture?, what human know so far and what is my new theory or idea of human have nine senses my knowledge about my topic which is middle childhood development with additional senses I add in human being in general psychology is the focus of this book.

• Additional senses we must teach it to adulthood development are.

• Sense of sex:

• This sense is growing understanding from early age and they must be research more about this important sense. For example, what age we must start to teach this sense to boys and girls. What should be learning for this sense of human being is very important. Also sense of sex is not related to faith or sin and is human nature and even animal have it and they don't talk about the faith or sin or devils, or angels which all baloneys. It is most important things we must teach separation of human being and religion in human body and science of human being. I see Kids suicide in teenager time is miss understanding of sin or faith with religion can cause bad behaviors. We must make sure those senses are anatomy of human and we must understand of all human senses.

SEX PROBLEMS

• Early marriage or early age pregnancy all problems are in societies with confusion and miss understanding. In my experience sense of sex must be started as soon as learn to talks and use of computer with basic knowledge of them self for boys just about sense of sex organ and for girls also just for sex organ and in middle childhood with solo playing for kids . It is very important to understand this sense not a sin or shame for children and it is part of body to satisfying this sense of human. Parents must be teaching this sense separately to (Boys, and Girls) children, and this process must not start until age 5 years. If kids, go to preschools parents also teachers must be to teach the deference's of males and females with basic physically and mentally differences to children. As soon as they can read and write and research in internet, parents and teachers must teach basic knowledge of sense of sex and solo playing. How they can play with themselves without thinking about the sin or shame and satisfy these senses in right way of secure privacy with right analyzing of opposite sex in educational video or pictures. To teach right way with good behaviors, are most important subject. Children and parents must understand of love and opposite sex in early childhood development. Teaching basically, basic love is most important, and roses for love, to make sure to teach the values without having any sex intercourse until 18 years old. Just watching video or pictures and to understanding of laws and regulation in society are the key to having healthy environment and society, with satisfy children especially in middle age of childhood or teenager times.

SENSE OF SPEAKING AND RELIEF

• I been in European country or Asian country which adult they can buy the sex for 1 hours and those country have better understanding of complexes and jealousy's and sex are better than drug and smoking or drinking and those society has less violence and less crime. I recommended to United States with good healthy person and societies also with laws watching

for all adult men or women it can be ideal society.
- Sense of relief:
- This sense is like the other senses from early age kids will learn how to control, how to enjoy foods, and when they can relief of digested foods. Basic knowledge of this sense can direct the humans and all our children to right direction. Of course, use of this sense is a way to not to go in the wrong direction in sex activities and possibility of sicknesses and dirty condition and sickness of dirty hole, desists like Aids or other sickness education.
- Sense of speaking:
- Without communication human being can't say his or her needs and this sense it is one of the most important senses that can brings the human being in very high level of career today. If we can teach to our kids, how to speaks properly, how to explain things well, how explain his or her needs, how to sings or how-to defendant her or his self from very early age it is the key to success. This speaking sense is a life saver and it is most important sense to have good careers and today's problem solving.

SENSE OF SOUL OR TELEPATHY

- Sense of soul, telepathy, love, or hate:
- After we teach to the kids all senses which we must teach them in early age combination of all senses travels to brain and kids have a feeling of love or hate. Of course, these early loves are for parents and a child, will learned values about different religions or faith they will build a foundation of behaviors, cultural and values, which will effect children and adults to good images for decision making.

- Why my topic is so unique and important to the world of psychology, what is childhood needed for those changes, and what is the suggestion for those changes it is challenging of explanations.
- Understanding of all natures of problems is important in general psychology educational learning process in human being. To understand and to analyze all aspects of this new vision of human body and senses it is most important childhood development.

IDEA ABOUT HUMAN SENSES

- Idea about human senses is so powerful that can change the psychology in all phases of human being behaviors. I believe humans have 9 senses verses six senses we used to learned. This theory will be revolutionary Idea in psychology and will be change the educational psychology especially in early childhood development. Understanding of human anatomy and relation to any hole in body we have, to clarify all humans have those same holes we can see and feel. All nine senses of human being which makes perfect men and women is to be understanding of human senses, in general psychology.
- The value of this Idea of human has 9 senses will be changing the structure of the educational learning on any acts in psychology they can be imagine. I must analysis all my research around this educational general psychology for solving problems in society are based on my experience and my expertise with a little bit effort on other related researches. Also, I can achieve my goal to write this assignment foe middle childhood development

TREATMENT IN LIFESPAN

- Some treatment in lifespan:
- In conclusion of our patient kid's or adult who are on the risk for substance abuse in the form of alcohol or smoking in take as a mental and physical health problems?
- To see adult Problems and foundation of what he learned from early childhood to late adulthood is the solution of his treatments, which I think still it is not too late caught up with adult to enjoyment of his, or her life. we must help all adult financially and mentally and take long vacation with wife, or husband maybe without pay and look all aspect of the life again. Adult must enjoy the life what he, or she has, and to have enough to take a good judgement and I think they doesn't need counselling. Some people are work alcoholics and must take a break and see the life better, which I think adult's is working too much.
- I encourage all adult to relaxation to learn about Human has nine senses with techniques and use a mediation and exercise are his goal. This theory, which is not only the opinion it is a fact of human being that we must understand of human holes and relation to senses.

PSYCHOLOGY

• This theory will change the science of psychology in all phase of human behaviors. Aim of this case study was to answer relationship between adult and environment, with cultural differences, language differences, and race and gender differences, how we can with strategic plan solving educational system about behaviors and learning human senses in adulthood development. To analysis strengths and weakness of this research and my idea or my theory of human has 9 senses, which was focus of this paper. I am confident if my goal is to teach parents and teachers with disciplinary action human has 9 senses, it will solve lots of problems in childhood and adulthood development for lifespan. This dissertation will be educational learning experience on general psychology for childhood and adulthood development. I hope I did my part of duty to be in this world of science. To understand and solving the problems like, Hyun-Ki's, and Tayib's, Dave's, Majid's , Ali's Mike, Sally's , Sarah's in all cases in society or family we need to understanding, human have nine senses and all human in the earth speak same language, with same values and cultures.

CULTURAL DIFFERENCES

•Cultural Differences:
•Becoming a psychologist, therapist in culture and to sorting different culture to the test always is complex and challenging. To identify my culture before I was in United State, there were process of transformation, and educational learning experience. I saw different stage of my lifespan was shaped with confusion and different fundaments, which might be struggling with my mind. As I am passing through different neighborhood, different ages, different race I saw different cultures are hard to understand. I saw some stereotype people in society with different race, nationality different wealth, religious, genders, sexual orientation, etc. Also, in my study, I did view of Hay's article (Hays 2008). She said the first stereotype mentioned were racial identity (Hays 2008). Addressing different culture in today's world is relatively facing a lot of issues with ethical dilemma and consequences in societies. We must as a future therapist diagnoses and find a treatment for someone with confusion or psychological problem about culture. We are all facing new people in town with new cultures which new personality has been facing culture shook with some stereotype of background. Ethical problems and bad behaviors we see in every single day in societies are today's problems.

CULTURE

•African American, Asian American, European American, Australian American, Mexican, etc. all have some angry issues about each other in some point, in case of cultural differences. Some viewing about religious or history they leaned or racial identity or about skills they learned, or some about cultures they learned, the way they talk's or the way walk, or eat, or dress which cause dilemma. Cultural differences or cultural shook's is real and misunderstanding of new culture can cause behavior problems. I am going to discuss those issues with what I learned from past to present and what is good for future of cultural identities for societies.
•According to APA (2010), "psychologists planning to provide services, teach or conducts research involving populations, areas, techniques or technologies new to them undertake relevant education, training, supervised experience, consultation or study."
•Objectives,
•When we are conducting research about cultural identities what is stereotype Hays states that: "People are often surprised by how many stars- that is, how much privilege- they have."
•Also, Hays, P.A. (2008). Suggest into the clinician's Mirror: Cultural self- Assessment, Addressing cultural complexities in practice: Assessment with Diagnosis, and Therapy (2nd Ed.)
•To read and having experience to live with different cultures in world, I must admit we need new vision of the world and mixing all cultures to one good one. I find out in our discussion based of my experience and see the world stereotype , what we know is wrong past about religious or race or nationality, etc. all can be wrong information, we must understand who really, we are, and who is real human being. How we can build a real human being for new world to make us a perfect human. To understand of humans needs we need a vision of past, present and future humanity. Humans can make a sense of those important in cultures and be happy with joy together. Which I have to say," life is short, and we must enjoy time in the world."

CULTURAL IDENTITY

- Evaluate own cultural identity,
- Also, I have to say I am not proud, I had Asian culture background, or I lived in Europe, and I learned Europeans culture, or I am right now in American and I have learned American culture. I see all cultures have imperfection and all those cultures are not for real human being. We are all Stereotyping in some point, past race, past religious, or past sexual orientation, etc. which were all of them wrong in some point and I have very strong rejection to all wrong history and past learning experience. I see all cultures have failure because of complexity of wrong past information. We must know history was wrong because of lack of discovery or innovation and science. We should know we don't need to follow past religious history because there was not true. For example story of Noah prophet, which I mention in my book, "Legal Concept of Law and Human Behavior Senses"(2009). I said all religious have same wrong information of world and story about flood, which was wrong. We learned discovery of America which was about 400 years ago, and in the time of Noah which was 5 to 10 Thousand years ago , they didn't know world was flat or round and Galileo discovery of world was only 400 years ago, and church called Galileo crazy man and they poison him. We still teach those histories which is wrong in school and to our children which our kids can take a world to wrong direction. They said world was flood it, which were wrong. They find a bone of dinosaur million years ago in Arizona and there was not under the water, and we can see those bones in museum today. Also we see those stereotype people in today's world. They build a Noah Arc in Kentucky recently to make more money to advertising wrong messages, which is stereotype. I am just a free man to tell you truth and we see some hard head people or stereotype don't buy the reality and they said you are communist, and they don't face reality. Most problems in the world are about religious, which all past information were wrong in my opinion because of lack of science and innovations and discoveries and all lying to us about the past.

LEADER ADVICE

- Discuss the importance of multiculturalism and diversity in ethics and general psychology,
- History offers numerous illustrations of the importance of culture for any nation using past leader's advice or counsel or customs tools effectively to build a foundation for culture. Works of such leader like Moses, Jesus, and Mohammad lay the groundwork for creating cultural system of behaviors for humanity and multiculturalism of today's general psychology. During the time we must change those roles. Culture is deep in human behaviors. In some east cultures, said good cultures must possess four qualities:
- 1-Justice, 2- Intelligence, 3- patience, and 4th- Modesty
- Conversely, and good culture must never possess the four vices:
- 1-Envy 2- Arrogance 3- Narrow- mindedness 4- Malice
- This was the dominate lesson of good culture in time of wisdom, which I think we lost those advice during the time and we must learn it again.

GENERAL PSYCHOLOGY OF HUMAN SENSES

- Identities and examine competency of multicultural in general psychology,
- United States is one of the biggest nations with multicultural societies which Law protects the citizen with good foundation of constitution. General psychology in United States is different from rest of the world and for example freedom of writing or speech, or dress, or food and drinks is unbelievable in U.S. compare with some Asians, Africans, Europeans, or Australian countries. For example, during months of Ramadan people in my country cannot eat or drink in publics and they may go to jail or punished. People cannot dress casually or what they want. Reading any books or write any things, etc. are against those laws.
- Making common sense of multicultural world to practice perfection,
- For generations, the wrong information has been taught by parents and schools alike, for example the human being has five senses, which is not true. My theory human has nine senses will change the psychology and cultures. Human has several holes and all opening related to human senses, like ears, eyes, month, there are two more holes in the body one in front- the vagina for female and penis for male which is sense of sexuality. And hole behind human is senses of relief provided an exit for digested food which are 2 additional senses. Also, human can make a noise with voice box located

at the base of the throat. Therefore, the voice the ability to make a sound and speaking is other human senses, and sense of speaking. Which those additional senses teach to our kids can change the culture and it will be revolutionizing the all aspect of human behaviors and psychology (M. Khodabandeh 2009). I am hopping this Idea will change all cultures of the world base on real human being.

HUMAN SENSES CULTURE

•Conclusion, looking for next 1000, years to test the culture,
•Vision of culture is the process of creating good cultural ideal for future state. To make sure is preparing, shared and understanding all cultures. New Culture must be view with clear mind and good emotional balance of understanding values and freedoms. Human culture must manage understanding of those different situations.
•Ideal culture is about a group of people that have same customs or roles for activities for sadness or for happiness, while sometimes found to be true for some people, and are over generalized as a common trail (Hays 2008). Also, Hays reports that stereotypes are often used to exclude others and usually are separate from other cultures or values. Some people used stereotype in negative ways with bad cultural issues which we see it in news every day like roles of religious about burton, gays, terrorism, etc.
•It is important to see the cultures in world more accurately, and what does good culture look like? What does bad culture look like? If, humans can manage to sharpen a pen for writing a good culture with clearer experiences for future references. Hopefully, psychologist can manage to write good culture for whole world base on humanity and right psychology.

REFERENCES

- References:
- American Psychological Associations (2010). Ethical Principles of Psychological and code of conduct.
- Alexander, R.J(2005, July). Culture, dialogue and learning and learning: University of Durham, UK.
- Allen, P.B. (1995). Art is a way of knowing. Boston, MA: Shambhala Publications.
- Carter, L.D. (2015). Reflecting humanity: Biological, psychological, and sociological perspectives (2nd ed.) Dubuque, IA: Kendall Hunt.
- Cohen Z. E. & Appelbaum P.S. (2016). Experience and opinions of forensic psychiatrists regarding PTSD in criminal cases. The journal of American academy of psychiatry and the Law.
- Broderick, P.C.,&Blewitt, P. (2015). The life span: Human development for helping professionals (4th ed.). P14. Boston, MA: Allyn & Bacon.
- Boske, C. (2011). Audio and Video reflections to promote social justice. Multicultural education technology journal, 5 (1), 70-85.
- Bonner, B.L. (2004). Expertise in group problem solving: Recognition, social combination, and performance. Group Dynamics: Theory, Research and practice, 4, 277-290.
- Bray, R. M., Kerr, N.L. & Atkin, R.S. (1978). Effects of group size, problem difficulty, and sex on group performance and member reactions. Journal of personality and social psychology, 36, 1224-1240.
- Capella University(2014). programs of research department of psychology school of social and behavioral sciences retrieved May 28,2015
- Craig, Wendy M. (2010). The relationship among bulling, victimization, depression, anxiety and aggression elementary school children.
- Fogel, Allan (2011). Body sense. University of Utah in Salt Lake City.
- Min Kyu Kim (2015). Models of learning progress in solving complex problems expertise development in teaching and learning. (pages 1-161) April(2015).
- Hays, P.A. (2008). Looking into the clinician's Mirror: Cultural self-Assessment, Addressing cultural complexities in practice: Assessment, diagnosis, and therapy (2nd Ed.). Washington, DC: American Psychological Association.
- Khodabandeh, M. (2009). Legal Concept of Law and Human Behavior senses, Amazon.com
- Rones, Nancy(2009). Your baby's developing senses parents.
- http://www.search proquest.com.library.capella.edu/docview
- Ruscio, J. (2006). Critical thinking in psychology: Separating sense from nonsense. (2nd. Ed.).
- Sokol, J.T.(2009). Identity development throughout the lifetime: An examination of Eriksonian Theory. Graduate Journal of counseling Psychology, Vol. 1(20).

- Wowara, S.A.(2007). Introduction to the special issue: Academic dishonesty. Ethics & Behavior, 17(3), 211-214

LEGAL CONCEPTS OF LAW AND HUMAN BEHAVIOR SENSES.

•Human being from past to present and to the future.

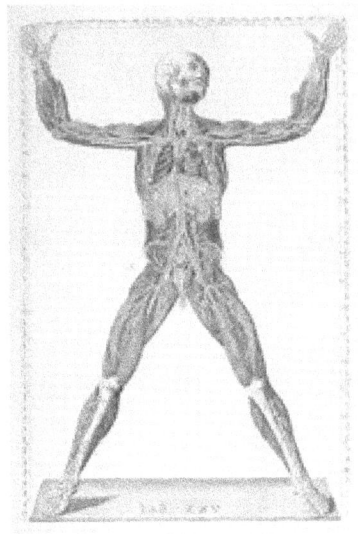

CAP ECONOMY

Cap Economy for saving the world

By Majid Khodabandeh
2020
My name is Majid Khodabandeh

PSYCHOLOGY BASED ON HUMAN HAS 9 SENSES
MAJID KHODABANDEH

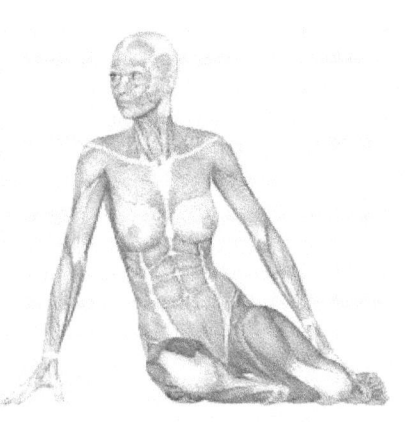

CAP ECONOMY

- I am 60 years old, older than
- Moses when he wrote the 10 commands, and I have a view of more than 6 thousand years history of the world with travelling and be in different continent, which most leaders in past didn't do it. All prophets just traveled only few cities. Also, prophets ridding with donkey. I am older than Jesus, who was only less than 36 years old with all his story and his issues, I am older than Mohammad which when he was died, he was around 60ths with all his story and his issues. I am older Karol Marcs, and Lenin with communist idea and new world on his time which everyone makes same wage or minimum wage with his idea and his issues. I am older than Gondi and his nationalism idea and his story and his issues.

CAP ECONOMY

- Also, I am older than all human being or statue or machine already they build it. All writers or story about statue build for several months like story of Buda or any handmade figures are fake. all those stories are fake with fake figure and fake news and all laws for those country made by human with lack of experience and knowledge of reality. Also, which those wisdom was less than 60 years old when the wrote his story and his, or her issues. I am, as a human being with long journey from Asia to Europe to America was be reliant experience with mazing learning experience which I want to share it to you all. Also, I believe you as a human being can be a prophet and perfect human being. like all history wrote so far, fake news there are all over the world to manipulate the innocent people. we as human and some as a writer must be careful and not aggregate the writing which it is not reality and fact. Most writing in past were wrong news and aggregate feeling of writing too much.

CAP ECONOMY

During my life I saw and lived in Dictatorships countries, Socialism, Communist countries, I was in Capitalism, Kingdom, religion government countries. I studied Architecture, ant apology, social ology, geology, civil engineering, city planning, public admi. Laws, business, I was self-employee, deal psychology at work and social works and studies of human behavior, etc. I did lean a lot and see all different political and social events and activities. I saw perfection and un perfection. I saw to many peoples goes up and so many people come down from power. I saw too many businesses open and close, too many government changes. I saw many changes in world from kingdom to socialism or dictatorship to commonest from capitalisms to socialism or kingdom to religion government. I saw changes from communism to religion.

CAP ECONOMY

I saw All politician who are someone looking for own pocket and run for political office, whom are not very nice and just talking and used one of the human senses too much. politician elected by the people to take chairs and nothing do after they are in the office and just lie to public and used the sense of speaking too much. All those politician and people who follow them look like it cannot make it right decision. Usually all politician or economist peoples with idea lass for several years and people they get tired of those rules, after a while and wants to change again to new idea or different party. Look like it Humanity needed always changing but is reality human needed are never changed for this 5 things, food, home, transportation, love, and communication devises if politicians follow this need for future generation with safety for all. If people need more work done, they leave me a question for me If people ask for new reform or revolution or codetta can solve human needs, are those needs are obvious and we don't need revolution or get crazy. I asked again If these needs are in any country difference from USA or all the same. if politician must provide all basic needs is necessary to survival and make it comfortable for all humans. we as a human we must not go too far for needs and unnecessary needs. We usually most the time we see we are going to the wrong direction. we think needs are endless for humans and luxury add in daily life. But all humans need are just food and housing, love, transportation and communication devise. My Idea about Cap economy is very simple and easy to understand and is necessary to survive in today's world. we have so far controlled the wealth for humans and balance the humanity with wealth.

We must somehow control and balance the wealth for people with laws and understanding of human behavior with psychology. one person cannot go wild and take advantage to others for greed or wrong market unbalance.
we must look for human success and capital wealth with the vision and cap economy. To have cap for healthy economy we must for any position put cap to everybody as human equality and equal opportunity is the key to new world. We must have peace and equal humans balance wealth and even up the world with raise the men, and women. It is always good perfect human and with freedom to grow and explore to the highest point of humanity with freedom. good human is to have all freedom right to choose protect women and children, handicap, and older people. To have a handicap, and older people.

SUPPORT ALL HUMANS

To have a vision and to see the limited world what we have we must share. To have a cab economy in every position we must have a sense of equal with freedom and no one can take advantage of the other take more than they needed. To have equal opportunity we must balance thought of parities' which we must have supreme cap economy job court.

Supreme cap economy is for set of the wages for all jobs, gov., or privet, nonprofit or profit companies from regular labors to CEO. Or president or owner. we must decide in this important issue. This cab economy still makes a capitalism and raise the humans in any phases and opportunity is endless for any job. For Example, like military person start for very basic major to all the way to general. Other example in grocery or retails we have cap for every 22.00 dollars per hours is the cap which usually after 5 years in the position they receive the 22 $ cap and after that no more raise is different department or different position with the new supreme economy cap provides to retails and all other businesses. My idea is going to every job from top to the bottom even in sport and CEO and all manager and business owner or corporation everything must have a cap there are all nation and world wealth is in hand of committee and no one can exceed more than they needed. Which if human's greed is control, wealth can be destroy others and one person or family or even nation can destroy the others or even world when no control the wealth. Humanities, small or big can be all kinds of dictatorship in small level or big level which can cause damage freedom and democracy. one person cannot have more than his or her needs. Cap economy control the wealth to all, which they offer him or her basic needs and even wealth. one they can't have mullite million dollars and someone cry for mercy.

Cap economy means what is highest paying in the nation person can make, like a minimum wage we have a maximum wage too. Person cannot make more than maximum wage in private or government profit or nonprofit which we must create committee which are 16 persons selected every 2 years by public for all jobs, from different businesses and different back ground and education and with experience make goal base on economy of the year set of the minimum wage and maximum wage in any businesses and one person wealth. We must put the Cap for any person, like CEO maximum they can make for example is 1 million

CAP ECONOMY

We must put the Cap for any person, like CEO maximum they can make for example is 1 million in the year. football player highest they can make 200,000.00$ a year. Owner of the business or businesses make 400,000.00$ for each business. President, or owner of the company can make up to 2 million.
these are including all bonuses and extra money. cap economy is control person wealth to balance the world with freedom and capital also with grow of economy and wealth to everyone in world equal. In cab economy rest of the money and profit for company goes to cap investment for whole nation and this rest of the money from businesses goes to build a hospital or school or university, road and bridges, etc. to subsidized for low income. This extra money is cap inv And is extra from taxpayer and we can lower taxes for people to, this cap inv. We Can pay student loan and health care to everyone. This extra budget from taxes and this extra money we can call it green budget, or cap investment.

This Cap Economy will balance the wealth for people with freedom and healthy economy which we can call it green budget.

Also, will cause the businesses to add more money given to all other employees also created more middle class in world and less economy problems for which Cap Economy is the key for healthy economy? I published the book" world language" which I discuses about 32 hours full time works for week job and add more money to employees' pocket or more hourly wages.

What they were making for 40 house changes for same money for 32 hours works. To have Cap Economy which we must set of the committee and research continuing years after years for make a new decision based on economy which provide every year to any nations and will eventually make it global cap economy for world base of cost of living and living expenses and wealthy nation and wealthy world.

International Agriculture Cap Economy.

To have a view of the past to present and future of the world we learning to feed the public always is big responsibility to any nation which was in the past on farmers solders which we want to make it more to organization has a employees with international view of hunger and needs with variety of foods and healthy chooses to everyone.

To have a vision of the world lands and rains and climate we can send a motorize farm equipment to plant and grows fruits, grains, crops, frozen food and farm animals like chicken, turkey, sheep, caw, pigs, fish etc., for every human been and no hunger anymore. Food they can sell it in market cheapest they can make and make subsidized some prices for necessary foods like bread, meats and cheeses, and vegetables, etc.,

Every state has own agriculture organization and working with other nation which has a same climate. university professor and student that do the research and go travel and co-op in different country or in the state must build a housing in next to the farm land for engineering and students and equipment approbator and regular labors workers with seasonal travelling and cultivating the croups and produce foods. All employees we must pay all of them fairs with free food and housing during the mission. I recommended all student with research and close university watch and homework's and learning from screech and move to the leadership and high pay with good retirement.

Building housing materials control and try to teach the people to builds own house.

Car factory and transportation cheapest can be with variety of chooses and with cap economy.

How wrong religion or fait can direct the economy in wrong direction or fake economy are must be watch carefully.

We must consider faith is imaginary and not reality. to believe on god and having some imaginary love or faith make an economy imaginary and fake too. We must go with reality and with science.

Prevent any fake economy specially with cap economy we must look everything year to years and go with reality of life.

CAP ECONOMY

History as I told in my book, legal concept of the law and human behavior senses. I said in my book Most of Story of geneses in old teas mend and Koran or Tora are wrong story and all this follower can have created wrong messages or fake economy. philosophy of communists is wrong too or Buda wrong too. Usually in world still teach in school story of Noah and world was flooded and to not knowing in Noah time, world was not discovering were round and goes around sun which Galileo discovered only 500 years ago and Noah was 5 thousand years ago. In Noah time they may be was in Turkey or Afghanistan rained for several days they thought whole world was flooded and technology was not strong enough to carry 2 elephants, 2 Greif of all the other animal and your family in one ship no

CAP ECONOMY

America was not discovered. There is other story like Adam and eve which they said Adam and eve were first humans, and philosophy were wrong if Adam was first human; he must steep with her daughter or eve sleep with his son for more population. which are wrong story and wrong philosophy with they take an economy or cap economy in wrong direction which must be with reality and day to day life, and no fake news Jesus come back to save you or Moses or Mohammad or Imams zaman come back to save you and wrong news.
People must understand of needs and what is reality of life and must work on it to make an economy strong and make a right decision. We must understand human life less for almost maximum 100 years not more and everyone will have died. To have a cap economy we have strong economy with equal opportunity and equal right with freedom and wealth also, healthy economy.

CAP ECONOMY

Communist are wrong economy in new world and people must paid on experiences and education and they can choose the job they like and wealth they needed. equal opportunity equal pay for women and men and with freedom. Only economy we used they have a cap for any jobs and businesses and bosses or owners of businesses with committee and board of cap economy which has a research center and committee work on income of businesses and make a cap for any jobs or corporation or businesses and control by the peoples and freedom of constitution branch of government.
Socialism is wrong too in socialism countries we see government take money as a tax too much to pay for roads school, hospitals, etc. From model class which middle class right now in those countries are poor right now and struggling for bills and basic needs.

CAP ECONOMY

Those countries take away money and charge the too much taxes to pay nonworker people or handicap or older people a little bit which is not right. We must in new world everyone somehow works and control the health and activities and make money and help the economy in capital world and human is capital. Even everyone works at home we must create the job or assignment weekly for few hours as assignment to be life has a meaning. I wrote this book for promote the freedom and equal humanity to everyone with the vision of to grow with capitalism with the cap economy to save the world for generation after generation and no one can take advantage from others. If someone works hard and studies hard get experience and knowledge can raise to

•the top of the company or communities or cities or even countries.
•We must learn the human has 9 senses and to satisfy those human senses we have perfect human being. to satisfy all senses we must change the laws and psychology base on those senses with equal opportunities to everyone and equal human being with freedom and freedom to choose and open minded to cap economy.

CAP ECONOMY

CAP ECONOMY

CONTENTS

World Language 1

Introduction 2

Alphabet: 3

Numbers: 3

New Year: 4

Week Days 5

American, English, Australian 7

American Blue berry Pie: 12

Spanish: 13

Chicken Tortilla Soup 15

French 17

Beef Barley Soup 19

Italian: 21

Italian Four-Cheese Lasagna 24

Chinese: 26

Chines 28

German: 30

Germany 32

Farsi: 33

Japanese: 36

Arabic: 39

Russian: 41

Greek: 43

Hindi: 46

Southwest Black Bean Burgers 48

Brazilian(Portuguese): 50

Mushroom and Epazote Tacos 52

Turkish: 53

Ayran with Mint , or Yoguort drink 55

Cap Economy for Saving the World 57

World Language

Majid Khodabandeh

2020

Introduction

My Name is Majid Khodabandeh, U.S. Citizen , I was born in Tehran / Iran and I traveled all over the world and I live in Cincinnati Ohio, Northern Kentucky last 18 years. After many years learning different languages and knowing that if language you speak it is not your native tong there are always consequences that you are not 100% native on those culture and I feel, humans have a weakness, that they can not speak perfect language specially in the beginning of arrival to that country. I create this language for next generation and it is mix up of 18 languages with basic words that easy to memorize for all children to early adulthood and we add more vocabulary to childrens education. I recommend this book for every person. It is very good reference book and teach different cultures of language and it will bring the world together which human being in next generation will be speak in one language in all over the world.

I start In the Name of God who is still, missing and no one see or found him, and I will ask Who is really GOD is? We must try to know our self and knowing God with Technology and good knowledge of surrounding, to bring the God closer with imagination of having perfect world. I have to say life it is short and we must make the best of that for our time in the earth, to understand each other .We must believe on our self to communicate and understand the needs and live peacefully in the world.
 I must say God Bless you all, with kindest regards Majid Khodabandeh , I will present this book to all human being, make best for all of you and your family, community and country and make a giving of freedom bell rings, and protect freedom of writing and what we saying with the right words.
This book is World Language which will be use in all over the world.
Teachers and students, together in class rooms must read and memorizing all this words with repeated and again from kinder garden to 12 and this book will be the same, all the way to high school. School must have disciplinary action and spend every day at list for one hour to read and memorizing part of this book.
This book will improve the communication and open the boarders to other countries. Also, I encourage mixing the race and communication which will be improving humanity.
This book also provides a new culture and custom to follow with good humanity values.
I want to add also for each language one chosen recipe for favorite food of that culture at the end of each section.

Majid Khodabandeh
2020

Alphabet

A	B	C	D	E	F	G
Gh	H	I	J	K	Kh	L
M	N	O	P	Q	R	S
T	U	V	W	X	Y	Z

Numbers

1-ONE	2- TWO	3- CEH	4- FOUR	5- FIVE
6- SIX	7- SEVEN	8- EIGHT	9- NOH	10- TEN
11-ELLEVEN	12- TWELFE	13- CEHTEN	14 – FOURTEN	15- FIFTEN
16- SIXTEN	17- SEVENTEN	18- EIGHTTEN	19 – NOHTEN	20 - BIST
21- BISTONE	22- BISTTOW	23-	30- CEHI	31- CEHIONE
32- CEHITOW	33 – CEHICEH	34 – CEHIFOUR	35 – CEHIFIVE	36-
40- FORTY	41- FORTHYONE	42 – FORTHYTWO	43- FORTHYCEH	44 – FORTHYFOUR
45- FOURTHYFIVE	46-	50- FIFTY	51- FIFTYONE	52- FIFTYTWO
53- FIFTYCEH	54 – FIFTYFOUR	55 -	60- SIXTY	63- SIXTYCEH
64 – SIXTYFOUR	65-	70 – SEVENTY	80 – EIGHTY	90- NOHTY
100- SADD,	101- SADDONE	102- SADDTWO	103- SADDCEH	104 -

110 SADDTEN	111 SADDELEVEN	112 – SADDTWELF	113- SADDCEHTEN	114-
120 – SADDBIST	121 – SADDBISTONE	130- SADDCEHI	140- SADDFORTY	200- TWOSADD
300- CEHSADD	1OOO- HEZAR	10,000 – TENHEZAR	100,000 - SADDHEZAR	1,000,000= E' MILYON
1,000,000,000,= E' BILYON	1,000,000,000,000. = E' TERLYON			

New Year:

Months will be start of first of the season of spring which the called: 1st season. 21st day of old calendrer will be 1st of the months in new calendrer. Summer will be called: 2nd season , fall will be called: 3rd season and winter called: 4th season
New Year's will be with happiness celebration, big party and fireworks also after New Year's Day I encourage to visit all family and friends and neighbors during 15 days after new year.

	New name	old name	
		1st season, spring	
1st months:	Earth	Mar. 21St	
2nd months :	Tree	Apr.	
3rd months :	Human	May	
		2nd season, summer	
4th months :	Fish	Jun	
5th months :	Beef	July	
6th months:	Bread	Aug.	

3rd season, fall

7th months :	Peace	Sep
8th months :	Clean	Oct
9th Months :	Save	Nov

4th season, winter

10th months :	Happy	Dec.
11th months :	Rain	Jan
12th months :	Snow	Feb.

Week Days

New days name	old name	
1st day	Monday	
2nd day	Tuesday	
3rd day	Wednesday	
4th day	Thursday	off day
5th day	Friday	
6th day	Saturday	
7th day	Sunday	Off day

3 days off days employees have Which is one day of week will be employees' choice day off. Full time work will be 32 hours of works and everybody has three days off days. Minimum wage is 12.00 $ in 16 years after millennium and every 5 years add 1.00 $ more. Minimum wages base on American economy until world balance the economy in entire world. Eventually everybody will use same currency and will be global world economy. Global agriculture will be builded and no more hunger and everybody have work and transportation, shelter and food on the table with the right partner or wife or husband which must be easy access to everyone. I will encourage the partner not too much kids and maximum of 2 kids I recommended.

It is better in new world, we go with technology and every kid must have own computer and to stay home and do the homework's at home is best option. Study will be from elementary to high school, all on line school doing. There is no more spending to build a school, or university building, people don't have to pay school taxes and can improve the family economic. Student will receive the homework's on line and they don't need it to weak up early and drive the bus in cold or hot days. Freedom of time is most important and no more pressure for teachers or students to be in class room in early time of the day or dress code or to be in traffic to go to school. It also will be cut the violence in school and stress and will save a lot of money.

Most important things are for learning world language, we must know a little English language to start this world language which most kids in the world they know Basic English, so far and role of English. It will be in this book simplified English grammar and spelling and in most conversation and writing sentences will be complete with English words. We can complete the sentences with this book vocabulary, but we must use all of words in this book and we must mix the languages with variations of vocabulary. I wrote 150 wards or sentences for 13 languages which all of kids must learn these words during 12 years of school. It must be mandatory in schools or home schooling, by parents. Study of this book for 12 years with right pronunciation of each language is the key for success.

American, English, Austratian

English:

1-Where is she? 2- She's out side 3- she's eating
4- I walk to school every day 5- I run to school every day
6- I skip to school every day 7- I 'm going to school every day
8- The women were bitten by the dog
9- Which boy is in your class?
10- I didn't see Judy at the party. 11- There's a good restaurant down the street.
12- There's a drug store in the next block. 13- there are some new students in the class.
14- She may not have been there, 15- she had to finish a paper
16- John was not in class when it began.
17- He might not have been on time- 18- He over slept this morning

English

19- I got up late, so I didn't go to store for bread.
20- I'm going to buy a coat and hat tonight.
21- If we receive some money, we will go to New York City.
22- If we go to New York City we will go by plane.
23- He teaches the class every day. 24- Then he taught the class yesterday.
25- No he didn't teach it yesterday.
26- Why not? 27- She makes a cake every weekend-
28- Roya has a date every weekend
29- Majid makes a long-distance phone call every Sunday with his family.
30- Could you tell me the time? 31- Could you speak English?
31- Before you came? 32- Could you go tomorrow?
33- Could he come late? 34-Possibility
35- Could she cook before she was married?
36- Could you lend me a dime?
37- I write to my parents. 38- I will pay my bills by Monday.
39- I was going to study world Language.
40- The girl who is coming is my sister. 41- I was in Paris for 3 weeks.
42- The people likes to eat food. 43- May I have a drink or Food
44- Place the food on the table. 45- Give me a direction how I can find your house.
46- Somethings has been hidden in the house. 47 - what is it ?
48- Describe two hours of your life. 49- I can run as fast as Reza.
50- I can sing as loud as Emily

English

51- Hello 52- My name is 53- How are you 54- Nice to meet you
55- Thank you. 56- Good buy 57- Getting up in the morning
58- Eating breakfast 59- going to bed 60- lighting the fire
61- Going down the shaft 62- I a wake from sleep
63- I open my eyes 64- I look for my watch. 65- I find my watch

66- I see what time it is 67- It is six o'clock
68- I get out of bed 69- I put on my Pants 70- I put on my stockings and shoes
71- I wash myself. 72- I comb my hair 73- Put on my collar and necktie
74- I go downstairs 75- I open the door of my bed room.
76- We are getting warm 77- you are getting worm 78- they are getting warm
79- Mark wasn't driving, was he? 80- You weren't late, were you?
81- Excuse me for being late 82- I am sorry I am late.
83- I am sorry I forgot to come 84- (answer your letter) 85- Inform you
86- I had such a good time. 87- I hated to come back
88- Where were you last night. 89- what'd you get so angry at me for this morning.
90- What is a warranty? 91- I just move to here
92- Don't be so picky, we can fix that
93- Marital status 94- Interests 95- health 96- community
97- How should children be punished for misbehavior?
98- What are your feelings about homework?
99- What psychologist call the "by stander" effect" means
100- That Individuals are never willing to help out.

English

101- discuss 102- define 103- Talk about it = describe 104- a process
105- Concepts= description and summary 106- of course
107- She answered all the question 108- he jumps on the bus.
109- You ought to be more careful.
110- When the sea is calm, we go out in a boat.
111- This story is more interesting than that.
112- I look for my ruler but I can't find it .
113- They couldn't go by bus, so they went by train.
114- The weather was good, so the sea was calm.
115- It was his fault because he wasn't very careful.
116- I can't cut the string because I haven't a knife.
117- Cinema 118- to run away. 119- to run after
120- Whole 121- please blow out that candle
122- He didn't put the money in his pocket.
123- I didn't buy my sister a watch 124- the dog didn't run after the cat.
125- He didn't give her a piece of chocolate.
126- He was beginning to help his mother.
127- the children were laughing and shouting.
128- We were buying flowers at the shop.
129- She picked up the coins 130- the dog led a blind man across the street.
131- No, I forgot nothing, 132- never mind
133- Cheaper 134- I shall bring my things in a bag
135- He complained that it was cold.

English

136- Did you say that he was playing?
137- Lovely flower. 138- Will they buy a new car?
139- Will you come tomorrow? 140- Will he be very careful?
141- He looked everywhere for his hat.
142- Whistle 143- to take the penalty- kick.
144- Two goals to nothing. 145- You won't laugh when you hear this story.
146- We blow a whistle 147- he threw the ball through the window.
148- The bad man struck the policeman.
149- The cat was washing itself.
150- The nurse is tired because she has worked too hard.

TIME:1 hr
Prep: 20 min
Inactive Prep: --
Cook: 40 min
YIELD: 4 servings
LEVEL: Intermediate

ingredients

- One 10-ounce box frozen green peas
- 2 tablespoons cold unsalted butter
- Zest of 1 lemon
- Vegetable oil, for frying
- 2 pounds russet potatoes, peeled and cut into 1/3-inch-thick batons
- 2 cups all-purpose flour

English

- 1/2 cup rice flour
- 1 teaspoon baking soda
- 3/4 cup lager-style beer
- 3/4 cup seltzer or sparkling water

- 1 teaspoon lemon juice
- One 1 1/2-pound fillet hake, cut into 1 1/2-inch pieces (about 2 1/2 to 3 ounces each)
- Kosher salt and freshly ground pepper
- Malt vinegar, for serving

Bring 6 cups of generously salted water to a boil in a medium saucepan. Add the frozen peas and cook for 4 minutes. Reserve 3 tablespoons of the hot cooking water, and then drain the peas and return them to the pan. Immediately add the butter, lemon zest and cooking water and season with salt and pepper. Roughly mash the peas with a potato masher or in a food processor, and then cover and set aside.

Heat 2 inches of oil to 300 degrees F in a Dutch oven or heavy-bottomed wide pot. Meanwhile, rinse the potatoes with cold water to remove some of the surface starch and then dry well. Blanch the potatoes, in 2 to 3 batches to avoid overcrowding the pot, until just cooked through but still blond, about 2 minutes. Transfer to a paper-towel-lined baking sheet.

Raise the temperature of the oil to 345 degrees F. Preheat the oven to 200 degrees F. Whisk together 1 1/2 cups of the all-purpose flour, the rice flour, baking soda and 1 teaspoon salt. Pour in the beer, sparkling water and lemon juice and mix just until combined (do not over-mix). Keep the batter refrigerated until ready to use.

When the oil is ready, fry the potatoes in 2 to 3 batches until they are crisp and golden brown, about 3 minutes. Drain on a paper towel-lined baking sheet and sprinkle with salt, and then transfer to the oven to keep warm.

Sprinkle the fish fillets with salt and pepper. Coat the fish in the remaining all-purpose flour and then dip into the batter to completely coat. Carefully swish the fish partway into the oil for a few seconds before completely releasing. Once the coating starts to set on the first fillet, you can add another battered fillet into the oil. Fry until the fish is puffed, golden brown and cooked through, 5 minutes for thin fillets or 7 minutes for thick fillets, and then transfer to a paper towel-lined plate. Cook the remaining fillets and sprinkle with salt.

To serve, reheat the mushy peas if necessary. Serve the fish with the chips, mushy peas and malt vinegar on the side.

American Blue berry Pie

- Prep Time: 30 min
- Cook Time: 40 min
- Ready Time: 240 min
- Yield: 8 servings

Ingredients

- Double Crust Classic Crisco Pie Crust
- 7 cups peeled, cored, thinly sliced tart apples
- 1 cup fresh blueberries
- 1 tablespoon lemon juice
- 3/4 cup granulated sugar
- 1/4 cup firmly packed brown sugar
- 1/2 teaspoon ground cinnamon
- 1/2 teaspoon ground allspice
- 1/2 teaspoon ground nutmeg
- 2 tablespoons Pillsbury BEST™ All Purpose Flour
- 1/2 tablespoon tapioca
- 2 tablespoons butter

GLAZE

- 1 large egg white
- 1/2 tablespoon warm water
- Sugar

Preparation Directions

- PREPARE recipe for double crust pie, using a 9-inch pie plate. Roll out dough for bottom crust and place in pie plate according to recipe directions.
- HEAT oven to 425°F.
- TOSS apples and blueberries in large bowl with lemon juice. Add granulated sugar, brown sugar, cinnamon, allspice, nutmeg, flour and tapioca. Mix well. Spread evenly in prepared pie crust. Cut butter into small pieces and place on top of filling.
- ROLL out dough for top crust, place onto filled pie and finish edges according to pie crust recipe directions. Cut slits in top crust or prick with fork to vent steam.
- BEAT egg white with warm water. Brush on top crust. Sprinkle with sugar. Put a strip of foil around the edge of crust while baking to prevent excessive browning.
- BAKE 35 minutes. Remove foil; bake an additional 10 minutes or until crust is lightly golden and filling is bubbling.

Spanish

Spanish

Hola= Hello 2- Es'la disco= Table 3- Es'la Lampare = Lamp 4- Es'la Ventana= Window
5- No senor no es el televisor es el gato= no this not T.V , this is a cat
6- Es un lapis= pencil 7- Es un libro= this a book 8- Es la pizarra= This is a black board
9- Es un Mapa= this is a map 10- Una Pluma= This is a pen 11- un papel= Paper
12- La clase= Class 13- el profesor= professor, teacher. 14- Una mesa= student m.
15- el muchacho= boy 16- una alumna= student F. 17- una fruta= fruit
18- el avion= airplane 19- el cine= cinema 20- el perro 21- la cliente= customer
22- el pan= bread 23- el queso= cheese 24- las manzanas= apple 25- poco= keel
26- las botellas de leche = a bottle of milk 27- el padre la television= man watching T.V
28- los huevos= eggs 29- mucho= boy 30- grande = elephant 31- bonito= wining
32- trabajador= construction labor worker. 33- el aire= air 34- el ano= the year
35- la calle= the street 36- la cosa= the thing 37- el dinero= the money

Spanish

38- la flor= the flower 39- el hombre= the man 40- la mujer = the woman
41- la oficina= the office 42- el parquet= the park 43- la prisa= the hurry
44- la tienda = the store 45- alto, a = tall, high 46- extranoa= strange
47- grande= big, large 48- mucho, a = a great deal 49- sus = their
50- tanto, a = so much
51- el cumpleanos= the birthday 52- Buenos dias= hello, good day
53- bien= well 54- adios= good bye. 55- tanto, a = so much 56- to dos, as, = every, all
57- tonto,a = foolish 58- mira= she looks, at watches 59- son= they are
60- van= they go, walk 61- visita= visits 62- vivir= to live 63- una= a
64- el chico usa el libro = the boy uses the book 65- vecino= the neighbor
66- el nene= the baby , el nino= the child 67- go zar= to enjoy 68- pobre= poor
68- ocupado, a = busy 69- su= his, her, your 70- comprar= to buy.
71- escucnas= to listen 72- feliz= happy 73- dulces= candy 74- pagar= to pay

76- el cocae= the car 77- el equipo= the team 78-amable= kind
79- la opportunidad= the opportunity 80- bello, a = beautiful
81- libre=free 82- el animal= the animal 83- la biblloteca= the library
84- el billete= the ticket 85- diego= james
86- gracias a dios! Thank heaven! Thanks god

spanish

87- oir= to hear 88- cada= each 89- listo, a ready 90- abierto,o= open
91- toda la famillia= the whole family 92- de papel= of paper
93- de vidrio= of glass 94- azul= blue 95- que= which, that
96-la edad= the age 97- la hierba= the grass 98- ya= already
99-la ensalada de papas= the potato salad 100- volar= to fly
101- ilueve= it rains 102- mover= to move 103- al morzar= to lunch
104- nieva= it snows 105- elzapato= the shoe 106- la silla= the chair
107- la nariz= the nose 108- la escuela= the school
109- el future= the future 110- el idiota= the idiot 112- odiar= to hate
113- I pon! = put 114- la esposa= the wife 115- el risgo= the risk
116- la semana= the week 117- anda= you go, go
118- comprendo= understand 119- favorite, a = favorite
120- peligroso, a = dangerous 121- proximo, a= next
122- tanto= so much 123- escribir= to write 124- asi= such
125-juntos= together
126-sino= but 127- buen= good 128- el aceite= the oil
129-la esperanza= the hope 130-no importa= it dose not matter
131- el alma= the soul 132- la bodega= grocery store,
133- tuve= had 134- al menos= at least 135-el Fuente= the fountain
136- de casados= as a married couple. 137-morir= to die
138- tener mucha suerte= to be very lucky
139- ya no= not now, no langer 140- la piel= the skin

Spanish

141- la fama= the fame 142-esperar= to wait 143- excusar= to excuse
144- suficiente= enough 145- si que= in deed 146- to car= to play ,music
147- acordado, a = remembered 148- mentir= to lie
149- Buenos dias= hello 150- adios= good bye

Chicken Tortilla Soup

Prep Time
0
hr.
15
min.
Total Time
0
hr.
40
min.

Servings

6 servings, about 1 cup each

A Southwestern cousin of Mom's chicken soup, this one has a kick with a crispy topping. And, like its popular relative, it'll make you feel good all over.

what You Need

- 6 corn tortillas (6 inch), divided
- 1-1/2 tsp. oil, divided
- 1/2 lb. boneless skinless chicken breasts, cut into bite-size pieces 1 ea For $5.79 thru 03/01
- 2 cans (14-1/2 oz. each) chicken broth
- 1 cup TACO BELL® Thick & Chunky Medium Salsa
- 1 cup frozen corn
- 1 cup KRAFT Shredded Cheddar Cheese

Make It

- Heat oven to 400°F.
- Cut 2 tortillas into strips; toss with 1/2 tsp. oil. Spread in single layer on baking sheet. Bake 10 to 12 min. or until crisp, stirring occasionally.

- Meanwhile, finely chop remaining tortillas. Heat remaining oil in large saucepan on medium-high heat. Add chicken; cook and stir 5 min. Add chopped tortillas, broth, salsa and corn. Bring to boil; simmer on medium-low heat 15 min.
- Serve topped with cheese and tortilla strips.

French

1-Bonjour= Hello 2- Au revoir= good bye 3- la babe= baby
4- le nom= name 5-le pere= father 6- le cousin= cousin
7- la niece= niece 8- la vie – life 9- le marriage= marriage
10- bruns= brown 11- raides= straight 12- le teint= complexion
13- blond= fair, blond 14- brun(e)=dark 15- rire= to laugh
16- figure= face 17- le nez= nose 18- la langue= tongue
19- le menton= chin 20- le corps= body 21- le bras= arm
22- la main= hand 23- talon= heel 24- la balcon= balcony

French

25- premier e'tage= first floor
26- le mur= wall 27- le garage= garage 28- le salon= living room
29- la table= table 30- le tapis= carpet 31- le cheminee= fire place
32- la radio= radio 33- le four= oven 34- la gaz= gas
35- proper= clean 36- sale= dirty 37- la terre= soil
38- le nid= bird 39- le busson= bush 40- la tulipe= tulip
41- le bulbe= bulb 42- la rose= rose 43- la patte= paw
44-le lapin= rabbit 45- le bocal= bowl 46- la douche= shower
47-le savon= soap 48- nu(e)= naked 49- glace= mirror
50- se raser= to shave
51- la brosse= brush 52- le parfum= perfume 53- la cravate= tie
54-le tee= shirt= T- shirt 55- le chapeau= hat 56- les sandales= sandals
57- la balance= scales 58- la lampe de chavet= bed side lamp
59- le lit= bed 60- le bol= bowl 61- le pot= pitcher 62- le potage= soup
63- le dessert= dessert 64- le vin= wine 65- le bifteck= steack
66- le jambon= ham 67- la saucisse= sausage 68- la carotte= carrot
69- la tomate= tomato 70- cru(e)= raw 71- la salade= lettuce
72- le raisin= grapes 73- la fraise= strawberry 74- mur(e)= ripe
75- la prune= plum

76- le melon= melon 77- a mer or a mere= bitter, sharp

French

78- l' orange= orange 79- le yaourt= yogurt 80- le sel= salt
81- le riz= rice 82- les' epices= spices 83- la chocolat= chocolate
84- le biscuit= cookie 85- la patisserie= pastry 86- cuisine= cook
87- le disque= record 88-la musique classique= classical music
89- la journal= newspaper 90- le magazine= magazine
91- le journal illustre'= comic magazine 92- la poe'sie= poetry
93- le tissue= fabric 94- la galerie= art gallery
95-la collection= collection 96- chanter= to sing
97- les jeux(m)= games 98- la place= seat 99- danser= to dance
100- le restaurant= restaurant.
101- le garcon= waiter 102- commander= to order
103- le pour boire= tip 104- le plateau= tray 105- le zoo= zoo
106- l' addition= bill 107- le zebra= zebra 108- l' animal= animal
109- sauvage= wild 110- donner a manger= to feed
111- le gardien de zoo= zoo keeper 112- le parc= park
113-le pique- nique= picnic 114- le banc= bench 115- se reposer= to rest
116- le singe= monkey 117- le kangourou= kangroo
118- le lion= lion 119- le tigre= tiger 120- le gardien= park keeper
121- la grande ville= city 122- la ville= town 123- pont= bridge
124- le cimetiere= cemetery 125- la pharmacie= pharmacy
126-le sac=bag 127-petit= small 128- moyen= medium
129- grand= large 130- combine coute= how much is..
131- ca coute= it costs. 132- l' escenseur= elevator
133-la letter= letter 134- le colis= package 135- collision= collision
136- capot= hood 137- le navire= ship 138- le pilote= pilot
139- les bagages a main= hand luggage. 140-la pension= guest house
141- flotter= to float 142- moustique= mosquito 143- le bois= wood
144- la feuille= leaf 145- le chene= oak tree 146- le champ= field
147- le bureau= office 148- le representant de commerce= sale repress.fench
149- en bonne sante= healthy 150- facile= easy/ difficile= difficult

Beef Barley Soup

Prep Time
0
hr.
15
min.
Total Time
0
hr.
35
min.

Servings

6 servings, about 1 cup each

This hearty beef barley soup gets an added layer of flavor by the addition of cut up cheese just at the end—it melts right in.

What You Need

- 1/2 lb. ground beef
- 1 lb For $4.99 thru 03/01
- 2-1/2 cups cold water
- 1 can (14-1/2 oz.) stewed tomatoes, cut up
- 3/4 cup sliced carrots
- 1 ea For $0.99 thru 03/01
- 3/4 cup sliced mushrooms
- 1/2 cup quick-cooking barley, uncooked
- 2 cloves garlic, minced
- 1 tsp. dried oregano leaves
- 1/2 lb. (8 oz.) VELVEETA®, cut up

Make It

Tap or click steps to mark as complete

- Brown meat in large saucepan; drain. Stir in water, tomatoes, carrots, mushrooms, barley, garlic and oregano.
- Bring to boil. Reduce heat to low; cover. Simmer 10 minutes or until barley is tender.
- Add VELVEETA; stir until melted.

Italian

1-Del pane= (some) bread 2- dello zucchero= sugar
3-della frutta= fruit 4- dell' acqua = water 5- dei bambini= children
6- delle case= houses 7- ho bisogno di soldi = I need some money
8- ho bisogno di amici= I need some friends 9-agni= each, every, all
10-languages= l' inglese 11- la bellezza= qualities
12- il generale= titles 13- I soldi sono utili= money is useful
14- lo ho dei soldi= I have some money 15- intelligenti= intelligent
16-ci sonodegli student nella classe= there are students in the class room
17- I = io 18- you= tu 19- lo, we= noi 20- lui= he 21- lei= it 22- loro=they
23- lui m' ama= he loves me 24- lui l; ha vista= he saw her

Italian

25- miama, non mi ama= he loves me he loves me not
26-maria compra I libri= mary buys the book 27- maria li compra= mary buy them
28- hai I biglietti= do you have the tickets 29- non li ho= I don't have them
30- lui ce lo mostra= he shows it to us 31- ne ha? Do you have some?
32- lui ne ha bisogno= he needs some. 33- il suo libro= her book
34- il libro di maria = mary's book 35- le sue= his
36- le sue camicie= his shirts 37- una mia amica= a friend of mine
38- un tuo libro = a book of yours 39- si, e' mia = yes it is mine
40- mi vesto= I get dressed 41- vesto mio figlio= I dress my son
42- ti, t' = your self 43- mi lavo il viso= I wash my face
44- mi lavo= I wash my self 44- chi e? I o! who is it ?
45- sei tu! It is you! 46- vuoi una mano? Can I help you?
47- no grazie, faccio da me= no thanks I 'll do it
48- chie' ansioso? I o= who is worried? I am
49- chi arriva? Noi. Who is coming? We are.
50- I figli di maria stanno studianda quelli di silvia guardano la telvisione= mary's kids are studying, silvia's are watching T.V

51-lui e' quello che amo= he is the one I love 52- bianco= white
53- largo= big 54- rosa= pink 55- viola= purple 56- blu= blue
57- qualche= some 58- qualsiasi= any 59- meglio= better

Italian

60- una vecchia amica= an old friend 61- un acara amica= a dear friend
62- minore, il minore= smaller, the smallest 63- cattivo peggio, il peggiore= worse, the worst
64- grande- maggiore- il maggiore= greater, bigger
65- questa casa qui molto grande= this house is really big
66- quella macchina la' e vecchia= that car is old.
67- mio fratello si chiama franco= my brother's name is frank
68- suo padre viaggia molto= her father travels a lot
69- piacere mio= my pleasure 70- quanti libri hai? How many book do you have
71- che ora e' ? what time is it 72- che bella casa hai? What a beautiful house you have?
73- che compito abbiamo per domain? What homework do we have for tomorrow
74- primo= president 75- non so che fare= I wonder what to do.
76- gli student vengono da lute le parti= the students come from all around
77- ieri= when 78- qui= where 79- molto= how 80- non vedo nessuno= I don,t see any body.
81- non ho ne' tempo ne' denaro= I have neither time nor money
82- suona il piano Giovanni? Does john play the piano
83- canta bene maria?does mary sing well? 84- cantante= singer
85- ambulante= walking 86- seguente= following 87- il gatto= cat
88-i soprovvissuti= the survivors 89- il primo venuto= the first to arrive
90- il cane= dog 91- I fiori = flower 92-la posta= mail
93- la moto = motor 94- la bicicletta= la bici= bicycle 95- grigio= gray
96- giallo= yellow 97- nero= black 98- orancione= orange

Italian

99- I colori= colors 100- biglietti= paper money
101-monete (moh-neh- the) = money change 102- mattina (math-tee-nah)=morning
103- pomeriggio (poh-meh-ree-joh) afternoon 104- sera (she- rah)=evening
105-la note= night 106- il caffe+ coffee 107- il te' =tea 108-il pane=bread
109- il pepe= pepper 110- il sale= salt 111- la Chiesa (kee-eh- zah) church
112- il metallo= metal 113- il metro= meter 114- milione= million
115-la misura (mee- zoo-rah) measure, size 116- la moda= style, fashion
117- il museo= museum 118- il momento= moment 119- la montagna= mountain
120- native= native 121- necessario= necessary 122- nuovo= new
123- nord= north 124- normale= normal 125- l' ombrello= umbrella
126- l' ospedale= hospital 127- ovest= west 128- il paio= pair
129- il palazzo = palace, building 130- perfetto= perfect
131- il permesso= permission 132- sud= south 133- est= east
134- la polizia= police 135- povero= poor 136- la porta= door

137- il prezzo(preh-tsoh) = price 138- il problema= problem
139- pronto= prompt= ready 140- pronto! Hello(telephone)
141-la qualita= quality 142- signore= ladies, women
143- signori=men 144- ricco= rich 145- il rispetto= respect
146- serio= serious 147- simile= similar 148- la somma= total, sum
149- primo= first 150- ama= love

Italian Four-Cheese Lasagna

Prep Time
0 hr. 20 min.
Total Time
1 hr. 10 min.

Servings

12 servings

Wondering what kinds of cheese show up in this lasagna? You can count on Neufchatel, cottage cheese, mozzarella and Parmesan to make an appearance.

What You Need

- 1 lb. extra-lean ground beef
- 1 lb For $4.99 thru 03/01
- 1 onion, chopped
- 1 pkg. (8 oz.) PHILADELPHIA Neufchatel Cheese, softened
- 1 cup BREAKSTONE'S or KNUDSEN 2% Milkfat Low Fat Cottage Cheese
- 1 pkg. (8 oz.) KRAFT Shredded Low-Moisture Part-Skim Mozzarella Cheese, divided
- 1/2 cup KRAFT Grated Parmesan Cheese, divided
- 1 egg, beaten
- 1 jar (24 oz.) CLASSICO FAMILY FAVORITES Traditional Pasta Sauce
- 1 can (14.5 oz.) diced tomatoes, drained
- 1/2 tsp. dried oregano leaves
- 12 lasagna noodles, cooked

Make It

- Heat oven to 350°F.
- Brown meat with onions in large skillet. Meanwhile, mix Neufchatel, cottage cheese, 1-1/2 cups mozzarella, 1/4 cup Parmesan and egg until blended.
- Drain meat; return to skillet. Stir in pasta sauce, tomatoes and oregano; simmer 5 min. Remove from heat. Spoon 1 cup meat sauce onto bottom of 13x9-inch baking dish; top with layers of 3 lasagna noodles, 1 cup cheese mixture and 1 cup meat sauce. Repeat layers twice. Top with remaining noodles, meat sauce, mozzarella and Parmesan; cover.
- Bake 50 min. or until heated through, uncovering after 40 min. Let stand 10 min. before cutting to serve.

Chinese

1-bu'cuo'= pretty good 2- duo'= more, many 3-ga'o= tall- high
4- danshi= but 5- shao= less, few 6- yaobu(ra'n) other wise
7- lia'ng= cool 8- le= new situation le 9- e'= hungry
10- bie'= don't 11- la'o= old 12- you--- y'ou= both…and…
13-ca'ise=colour 14- bu… le= not…any more 15- hui= to return
16- zhi'= only 17- du' shu= to study 18- he'= and
19- ma'n=slow 21-me'n= door 22- hua'yua'n = garden
23- shu(ke) =tree 24- shu'ca'i= vegetables 25- shafa= sofa
26- beizi= cup 27-tang= sugar 28- chazuo= socket
29-We'ibo'lu= microwave 30-hua'cha' jasmine tea

Chinies

31-Ce'suo'= toilet 32- ya'shua'= toothbrush 33-nianji= age
34- shenti= health, body 35- huo'=good 36- pia'nyi= cheap
37- de'ng=etc. 38- bufen=part, section 39- ba'okuo= to include
40-shengyi= business 41- shebei= equipment, facilitier
42- chengre'n= to admit 43- mo'u= certain 44- gonggong= public
45- ha'o= good, he'n ha'o= very good 46- zui ha'o= the best
47- zhengcha'ng= normal, regular 48- luxing= to travel
49- yin= cloudy, overcast 50- na'nnu'= men and women
51- la'oshao= old and young 52- na'n= difficult
53-ge'n= with, and 54- yiqi= together 55- fa'nzheng= any way, in any case
56- da'o…qu/la'i= to go/ come to/ to arrive 57- yua'n= palace
58- qingchu=clear, clearly 59- a shi a da'nshi= it's a all right but…
60- you yisi= to be interesting 61- mu'= eye 62- si'= silk
63- shi'= food 64- ma'= horse 65- ni'ao= bird 66- bing= ice
67- yo'u=also, again 68- cu'n= inch 69- he'ng= horizontal
70-shu'= vertical 71-tian= field 72- cho'ng= insect
73- yu'= rain 74- gu'= bone 75- he'i= black, dark

76- yu'= feather/wing 77- sho'u= hand 78- chi= smile
79- huo' che'= train 80-weixia'n= danger 81- ta'o= set
82- ba'o=newspaper 83- fe'n= a copy 84- wa'iguo'= foreign
85- ba'n= half 86- me'i= not 87- zaijia'n=goodbye
88- tu= earth 89- ya'o= want 90- qu'= to go 91-yue'=month

Chines

92- ha'i= still 93- ni'= you 94- dianying= film
95-ge'- see 96- ya'n= speech 97- mu'=eye 98- re'n= person
99- da'o= knife 100- shu'=vertical(line)
101- tia'n= field 102- zhuanjia= expert 103- ma'i= to sell
104- ca'o= grass 105- shui'=water 106- xin= heart
107-e'r= ear 108- shi= food 109-we'n lu'= ask the way
110- yuan= far 111- ji'n= near 112- zhongguo ge'ming bowuguan=museum of revolution- china revolution.
113- defang= place 114- xin= letter 115- zho'ng= heavy
116- hangkong= airmail 117-pingxin= surface mail
118- xian= first 119- tie'(shang)=to stick(on) 120- dizhi= address
121-shouju= receipt 122- guitai= counter 123- we'I shenme=why
124- ding= top, peak 125- rilluo= sunset 126- xiwang= to hope
127-shi= poem 128- do'u= funny 129- wa'ng= to forget
130-diu'= to lose 131- huaiyi=to suspect 132-wenti=question, problem
133-ge'ge'= each- every 134- zu'=to rent, hire
135- zhiye'= occupation, fresh 136- ga'njue'= feeling, sense
137- xinxian= fresh 138- tongyi= to agree with 139- feng= wind
140-ding= to go against 141- duo= how 142- gudian= classical
143- tian= sweet 144- likai= to leave 145- liwu= present, gift
146- haha= haha 147- youyi= friend ship
148-zui=drunk 149- hong= red 150- kuaile= happy, joyful

Chines

Beef and Vegetable Stir-Fry

Prep Time
0
hr.
25
min.
Total Time
0
hr.
25
min.

Servings

4 servings

Very good! Will make this again! Great and quick! (Those are just a few of the accolades this beef stir-fry has received from cooks like you.)

What You Need

- 2 cups instant brown rice, uncooked
- 1/4 cup lite soy sauce
- 2 Tbsp. KRAFT Lite CATALINA Dressing
- 3/4 tsp. ground ginger
- 1 lb. beef flank steak, cut into thin strips
- 1 lb For $9.98 thru 03/01
- 2 tsp. cornstarch
- 1 pkg. (16 oz.) frozen stir-fry vegetables, thawed, drained
- 1/4 cup PLANTERS Dry Roasted Peanuts

Make It

- Cook rice as directed on package, omitting salt.
- Meanwhile, mix soy sauce, dressing and ginger until blended; set aside. Toss meat with cornstarch; cook and stir in large nonstick skillet sprayed with cooking spray on medium-high heat 3 min. or until done. Add vegetables and soy sauce mixture; cook and stir 3 min. or until sauce is thickened and vegetables are heated through.
- Spoon over rice; top with nuts.

German

1-guten morgen= good morning 2- guten abend= good evening
3-gute nacht= good night 4- auf wiedersehen= good buy
5- sind sie aus Manchester= are you from Manchester
6- arbeiten sie onne computer? = Are you working with your computer?
7-haben sie sechs kinder? = Are you found children ?
8 –fliegen sie nach berlin? = flying to berlin? 9 zimmer= room
10-haben sie jetzt mehr geld? = Now you have more money ?
11-zu=too 12-nacht= night 13- teuer= expensive 14-bath=bed
15- dushe=shower 16- hier=here 17-links=left 18-genug=enough
19-klein= small 20- nur = only 21- fru'hstu'ck= breakfast
22- von= from 23-bis=until 24- halb= half 25-tee=tea
26-oder=or 27- vor=before 28- café'=café 29-dann=then
30-essen= eat 31-einmal= once 32- tisch= table 33- gehen= go
34- heute= today 35- zentrum= center 36- bus= bus
37- es tut mir leid= I 'am sorry 38- alle= alles 39-fussball= football

German

40- koffer= suit case 41- neu= new 42- ach, du meine gute= good grief!
43- glauben= ich glaube= believe, I believe 44-spater= later
45- zuviel= too much 46- stuck= piece 47- brot= bread
48- ei, eier= egg, eggs 49- bier= beer 50- tu'te= bag
51- mich= me 52- genau= exactly 53- grosse= size
54- wer= who 55- net= nice 56- billig= cheap 57- wolle=wool
58-baum wolle=cotton 59- zeitung= news paper
60- sagen= say- said 61- warum= why 62- auf= on
63- papier= paper 64- bei, beim= at , at the 65- buch= book
66- kennen= to know 67- ihn, ihm= him 68- termin= oppointment
69- sache= matter, thing 70- danke= thank you 71- sicher= sure, certainly
72- naturlich= of course 73- interessant= interesting

74- zeit= time 75- wunderbar= wonderful
76- ein paar= a few 77- arzt= doctor 78- krank= sick
79-ach so= I see 80- oben= at the top 81- an= at
82- ausgang= exit 83- tur= door 84- vielen dank= thank you very much
85- hinter= behind 86-kirche= church 87- gemu'tlich= comfortable
88- unser'e = our 89- hund= dog 90- schmerzen= pains
91- kommen= come 92- eis= ice-cream 93- huhn= chicken
94- gemu'se= vegetables 95- obst= fruit 96- wasser= water
97- fertig= ready 98- niemand= nobody 99- lieber= rather, prefer
100- brat wurst= fried sausage

German

101- unter wegs= on the move 102- fahr karte= ticket
103- zug= train 104- rauchen= to smoke
105- ver boten = forbidden 106- brief= letter 107- kasten= box
108- foto= photo 109- see= lake, sea 110- beide= both
111- voll= full 112- zweimal= twice 113- weil= because
114- alt= old 115- hoffen= to hope 116- dass= that
117- erste= first 118- letzte= last 119- thank stele= gas station
120- schule= school 121- u-bahn= under ground
122- ampel= traffic light 123- wenn= if, when 124- uns= us
125- heiss= hot

126- flug hafen= air port 127- leute= people 128- mutter= mother
129- wie geht's ?= how are you 130- richtig= right
131- wohnen= live 132- sein= his 133- junge= boy
134- schreiben= write 135- nie= never 136- flug= flight
137- was ist los? = what is the matter? 138- ja= yes
139- flugzeug = aeroplane 140- wir= we 141- bitte= please
142- entschldigen sie = excuse me 143- sind- are
144- gutten tag= hello, good day 145- nein= no 146- leider= unfortunately
147- nicht= not 148- stadt= town, city 149- sher= very
150- fur= for, mehr= more geld= money

Germany

Prep Time

20mins

Cook Time

14mins

Total Time

34mins

Yields

3 Servings

Ingredients

- 1 box (9 ct.) Three Cheese Bagel Bites®
- 1 jar pitted Kalamata olives
- 1 jar roasted red peppers
- 1 jar sundried tomatoes in olive oil

Directions

1. Preheat oven to 425°F.
2. Dice the olives. Chop roasted red peppers. Remove tomatoes from oil and chop.
3. Remove bagels from package. Top each bagel with olives, red peppers and tomatoes. Bake at 425°F for 14 mins. Remove from oven, plate and serve.

Farsi

1-Abort = aghim 2- a bomb= bomb 3- absent= ghayeb
4- accuracy= deghat 5- accustom= addat kardam
6- acknowledge- shenakhtan 7- addiction= e'tyadd
8- adult= balegh 9- a fire= ah'tash 10- alarm- clock= sah'hat
11- ally= dost 12- amaze= ta'ajob kardan 13- a miss=nah'dorost
15- arrest= das'gir 16- arsenic= margeh' mosh
17- auction= hara'j 18- author= nevie'sandeh
19- awesome= mayeh hormat 20- baby= bat'cheh
21- bait= toh'meh, azyat kardan 22- barbecue= kabab kardan
23- bashful= tar'so 24-bastard= harom' zadeh
25- bath= shosteh' sho kardan
26- battle= nabbard 27- beggar= geh'da 28- bet= shart'bandi
29- blind= koor 30- blowzy= sheh'lakhteh
31- boss= ray'eiss 32- bow= kham'shodan
33- briefly= mokh'tasar 34- broker= dal'lal
35- buyer= khari'dar 36- butter= kar'eh
38- capital= sar'mayeh 39- chef= ash'paz
40- chop-house= restaurant= restaurant arzaan
41- citizenship= tah'bahi'yat 42- complex= peh' chi'deh
43-console=del'dari daddan 44-construction= sah'khteman sazzi
45- conviction= mah'ko'mi'yat 46-cottage= kol'beh
47- dangerous= kha'tar'nock 48- dead= mor'deh
49-despite= eh' ha'nat 50- disloyalty= bie' vaf'ie

Farsi

51- distinction= far'gh , emtiyaz 52- down pour= baran'degi zyaad
53- ear= gosh 54- eat= khor'dan 55- ensure= beh dast avardan
56- encore= do' bareh 57- enough= an'daazeh 58- baba= father
59- baba aob daad = father give a water 60-koja meri= where are you going

33

61- halet chetor= how are you 62- mie khari= buying
63- del= heart 64- dass= hand 65- feet= paa 66- an'gosht= finger
67- san'dalli= chair 68- miez= table 69- zamine= earth
70- khah'k =soil 71- keeh'ream = lotion 72- nah ghashi = paint
73- ghorse= pills, medicine 74- mehmaar= architect 75- rah randeh= drivers
76- pan'jareh= window 77- daar= door 78- farsh= rug
79- ceh' ragh= lamp 80- telephone= phone 81- exam=e'mteh'han
82- excretion= annn=, madfu 83- fag= jon moft kanden
84- falsely= do'roghi 85- fat= chagh 86- feeling= e'h'sas
87- fine= jar'rimeh 88- fishy= mash'kok 89-flower= gool
90- floor= kaff' otagh 91- fly= mah'gass 92-force= zoor
93- fountain= fah'fareh 94- free= azaad 95- frozen= e'akhzadeh
96- fuzzy= na' malom 97- game= baize 98- gather= jam kardan
99- geography= goghrafi 100- way= rah
101- good= khoob 102- grass= cha'man 103- half= nes'f
104- hat= koh'lah 105- almond= ba'dam 106- wallnuts= ger'do
107- psychology= ravan shenasi 108- dentist= dandan pe'zeshk
109- independent= es'tegh'lal 110- tree= de'rakht

Farsi

111- kiss= boos 112- chess= shat'ranj 113- lawyer= va'kill
114- landlord= sa'heb'khoneh 115- leaf= ba'rg 116- left= chap
117- right= roust 118- like= mes'leh 119- lunch= na' har
120- dinner= sham 121- make- up= aarh'yesh 122- map= nagh'sheh
123- miss= az dast dadan 124- money= pool 125- monkey= may'mon
126- numbers= shomareh 127- oil= ro'ghan 128- office= daftar
129- part= e' ghesmat 130- passion= hayeh'jon
131- pie- sherini 132- perfect= ka'mail 133- race= mo'sa'begheh
134- rent= e'h'ja'reh 135- roof= sa'ghf 136- round= ge'rd
137-salt= na'mak 138- save= nehjot 139- screw= pe'ch
140- seat= jah, sandalli 141- a man of sense= e'nsan e'h ba sho'ore
142- shoe= ka' fe'sh 143- sleep= khaab 144- slow= ah' hesteh
145- spring= bahar 146- stone= sang 147- tooth= dan'daon
148- under= zieer 149- ugly= zehsht 150- pot= dieeg

White Rice - How to Make Basic White Rice

Ingredients

- 3 cups basmati or long grain rice
- 8 cups water
- 2 tablespoons vegetable oil
- 1/2 teaspoon salt

- Prep Time: 5 minutes
- Cook Time: 40 minutes
- Total Time: 45 minutes

Preparation

Wash rice in cold water, Drain and place in large bowl. Add about 8 cups of warm water. Allow to sit for 2-3 hours covered.

After rice has soaked, drain and save 6 cups of the water.

Pour rice water into a medium saucepan and bring to a boil. Add rice and salt. Allow to cook for about 10 minutes. Remove rice from heat and drain.

Pour vegetable oil in bottom of saucepan, add rice, then 2 tablespoons of vegetable oil on top. Simmer on low for 20 minutes or until rice is done.

Serves 4-6.

Japanese

1-what time is it? = Nan- ji desu ka? (nahn- jee dess-kah?)
2-It is one o'clock= Ichi-ji- desu= (Ee-chee- jee- dess)
3-It is five thirty= Go- ji- han desu= (Go-jee- Hahn- dess)
4-What time do you leave? Nan- Ji Ni demass- Ka? (nahn-jee-nee-day-mahss-kah?)
5-I have no more time.?= Moh ji- kan ga nai desu? (Moe-jee- khan gah-nie-dess?)
6-Do we still have Time? Mada ji- kan ga arimass ka? (Mah-da –jee khan gah ah-ree- mahss-kah?)
7-1 day= ichi-nichi (e- chee- nee- chee) 8- I am going to stay two days= futsuka-kan tomarimass- (futes-kah-kahn toe mah- ree-mahss)
9-What day is today? =Kyo wa nan yobi desu ka? (k'yoe wah nahn yoe-bee dess kah)
10-I hate Mondays= watakushi wa getsuyobi ga kiraidesu= (wah- tock-she wah gate- sue- yoe-bee gah kee rye dess.)
11-But I love Fridays. = keredomo, kinyobi ga suki desu.=(kay- ray-doe-moe, keen,yoe –bee-gah ski dess.
12-Next year I am going to japan= rai nen ninon e ikimasu. (rye nane nee- hone eh ee kee mahs.)
13-Please sign your name here= koko de namae wo kaite kudasai= (koe-koe day nah- my oh kite-tay kuu- dah-sie.)
14-Are you Mr. Watanabe? = Anata wa watanabe- san desu ka?
15-We= watakushi- tachi-(wah- tock-she-tah-chee)
16-You= anata-tachi(ah-nah-tah-tah-chee)
17-Who? = Donate? (doe-nah-tah)
18-Who is it? = Donate desu ka? 19- what is it? = nan desu ka?
20- itsu (eet-sue?) 21- what do you want to eat? Nani wo ta be tai no desu ka?
22- where? = do ko? (doe- koe?) 23- where are you going? Doko e iki masu ka?
24-where is it= doko ni a ri masu ka? 25- yes= hai(hie)
26-no= lie(ea-eh) 27- hello= moshi-moshi 28- thank you= ariguto gozaimasu.
29- thank you very much= domo arigato gozaimasu (doe- moe ah-ree-gah-toe –go-zie-mahss)
30- don't mention it.= do I tah shi mashite (doe-ee-tah-she-mahssh-tay)
31- excuse me= sum imasen! (sue- me- mah-sin)
32- welcome= irrashaimase (ee-rah-shy-mah-say)
33- good morning= ohaiyo gozaimasu (oh-hie-yee-go-zie-mahss)

34- good night= oyasumi nasai 35- excuse me= I'am sorry= go me na sai

36- just a moment, please= chotto matte kudasai

37-It's hot, isn't it! = Atusui desu, ne !

38- What time is it ?= Nan- ji desu Ka ?

39- How are you?= O' genki desu ka? 40- Genki desu= I'am fine.

41- Do you speak English? = Eigo ga hanasemasu ka?

42- I understand a little= Sukoshi wakarimasu

43- Please wait here= Koko de matte kudasai

44- I am the bus driver= watakushi ga basu no untenshu desu.

45- please get ready quickly= Hayaku yoi shite kudasai.

46-show me your passport, please= pasupoto wo misete kudasai.

47- are you here on business? Shigoto de kimashita ka?

48- how many (pieces) do you have? Ikutsu arimasu ka?

49- that's fine. Thank you= kekko desu. Domo arigato.

50- shall I help you? Tetsudai masho ka? (tate- sue-die mah-show-kah?)

51-where do you want to go? Doko e ikitai no desu ka?

Japanese

52- head= atama(ah-tah-mah) 53- ear= mimi(me-me)

54- eye brows= mayuge(mah-yuu-gay) 55- eye= me(may)

56- nose= hana(hana) 57- lips= kuchibiru 58- neck= kubi(kun-bee)

59- hand= te(tay) 60- finger= yubi (yuu- bee) 61- leg= ashi

62-heart= Shinzo(sheen-zoe) 63- liver= kanzo(kahn-zoe)

64- kidney= jinzo 65- rear=o' shiri= back 66- apple= ringo(reen-go)

67- stomachache= onaka ga itai (oh-nah- kah-gahe-tie)

68- chicken= chikin 69- eggs= tamago 70- garlic=ninniku

71-grape= budo 72- green peas= gurin pisu 73- salt= shio

74- mustard= masutado

75- rice= gohan(go-hahn)

76- onion(s) = tamanegi (tah- mah- nay-ghee)

77- sugar= sato 78- soup= supu 79- toast= tosuto

80- vegetables= yasai(yah-sie) 81- spoon= supunn (su- punne)

82- fork= foku 83- knife= naifu(nie-fuu) 84- beer= biru

85- coco-cola= koka kora 86- milk= miruku(mee-rue-kuu)

87- this way please= dozo, kochira e (doe-zoe-koe- chee-rah-eh)

88-the bill please= okanjo kudassai 89- address= jusho(juu-show)

90- age= toshi 91- adult= otona 92- admission fee= nyujo ryo

93-air-conditioner= reibo 94- airport= kuko 95- all right(ok)= dai jobu

96-alone= hitori 97- answer= henji (hane- jee) 98- a partment= apato

99- appetizer= zensai (zen- sigh) 100- arrange (get ready)=junbi(junne-bee)

101- arrival gate= tochaku geito 102- as soon as possible= narube ku hayaku

103- aunt= oba- san(oh-bah- sahn) 104- back(of/behind)= ushiro

105- bad= warui 9wah-rue-e) 106- bad(taste) mazui(mah-zuu-ee)

107- bag= bagu(bah-guu) 108- baggage= nimotsu 109- bank= ginko

110- bar=baa(baah) 111- barber= tokoya 112- bargain sale= oyasu uri

113- basement= chika (chee- kah) 114- big= okii(oh-keee)

115-big car= ogata sha 116- blood pressure= ketsu atsu

117- book= hon(hone) 118- bread= pan 119- cash= genkin(gain-keen)

120- change(money)= o' tsuri (oh- t'-sue-ree)

121- channel (T.V) = chaneru(chah-nay-rue) 122- cheap=yasui(yah-sue-ee)

123- cheese=chizu 124- chicken=niwatori(nee-wah-toe-ree)

125- child= kodomo

126-food= ryori 127- city= shi 128- clock=watch= tokei(toe-kay-e)

129-close= shut=shimemasu(she-may-mahss)

130-deliver= todokemasu 131- early= hayai(hah-yie)

132-eat= tabemasu(tah-bay-mahss) 133- electricity=light=denki(dane-kee)

134-embassy= taishikan 135- elevator= erebeta

136-enjoy= tanoshimimasu 137- evening= yagata(yuu-gah-tah)

138-expense= hiyo (he-yoe) 139- fairway= feauei(fay-ah-way)

140- famouse=yume 141- far=toi(toy) 142- girl=onna= nook

143-foreign=gaikoku no(guy-ko-kuu-no)

144-free (no cost) =muryo(muu-rio) 145- gloves= tebukuro(tay-bua-kuu-roe)

146-headache= zutsu shimasu 147- hospital= byooin(b'-yohn-een)

148- husband= shujin 149- interesting= omoshiroi(oh-moe-she-roy)

150- jewelry= hohseki(hoeh-say-kee)

Arabic

1-I= anaa 2- you= anta 3- he= huwa 4- they=umaa
5- we= nahnu 6- they(m) hum(hamm) 7- first name= al –ism
8-Sex(m)(f)= al jins 9- place of birth= makaan al- wilaada
10-marital status= al- haala al- madaniyya
11- single= a' zab 12- Married= mutazawwij 13- passport= jawaaz safar
14- what day is it today= Maa- I – yawm
15- to night= haadhihi al- Layla (hazat –al- lyyla)
Arabic
16-next= al- qaadim (Ghadem) 17- 1st= al awwa
18-2nd= ath- thaani (ath- sunni) 19- on= ala
20-Is it going to rain? Hal satumtir 21- downpour= gha aim
22-what's the weather going to be like today/ tomorrow= kayfa sayakuun at tags al-/yawm
23-between…and…= bain…. Wa 24- middle= wasat
25-here/ there= hunaa/ hunaak
26- every where= fii kul makaan 27- under= tahta
28-nea= qurba 29- in front of= amaama 30- up= fawq
31- inside= daakhil 32- outside= khaarij
33-behind= khalf 34- at the front= fii al muqaddima
35- in the north= fii ash – shamaal 36- south= januub
37- west= gharb 38- east= sharq 39- push= idfa 40- funduq=hotel
41- information= maluumaat 42- police= shurta 43- full= mamluu
44- danger= khatar 45- hello= ahlan 46- welcome= marhabar
47- how are you= kayfa haaluk? 48- good luck= hazzan saiidan
49- thank you= shukran 50- say hello to all= sallim alaa…kum
51- who= man? 52- what= maadhaa(ma'za)
53- what is this? Maa haadhaa 54- where= ayna
55- which one? = ay waahid 56- when? Mataa?
57- where are you going= illaa ayna anta dhaahib (dh=z)
58- why= limaadhaa 59- could you= hal yumkin… min fadlik?

Arabic

60- do you have…? Hal laday kum…? 61- sure= akiid
62- yes of course= na am, taban 63- all right= tamaam
64- perhaps= rubbamaa 65- no problem= laa mushkila
66- that's all right= laysat mushkila
67- never mind/ forget it= laa tahtam/ insa dhaalik (dh=z)
68- well done! =ahsanta sun'an 69- not bad= laa basai
70- how awful= yaa lahu min a mrin kariih
71- I am fed up= anaa munzaij 72- this is no good= haadhaa laysa jayyidan
73- friend= sadiiq 74- I am single= anaa a'zab 75- flag= alam
76- I work in an office= a' mal fill maktab 77- food= ta'aam
78- forget= yansaa 79- free= hur (un occupied)
80- fresh= taazij 81- fruit= fawaakih 82- frozen= mujammad
83- gallery= bahw (saala) 84- gasoline= benzin
85- glass= zujaaj 86- grand father= jad 87- grilled= mashwii
88- grocer= baqqaal 89- hand= yad 90- hat= qubba'a
91- heal= yasma 92- heart= qalb 93- heat= haraara
94- heel (of shoe) = ka'b 95- here= hunaa 96- hire= yastajir
97- holiday= u tia(uot'let) 98- how long= kam al mudda
99- jack (for car) raafia 100- jaw= fak
101- jewelry= mujawharaat 102- job= shughl= wazifa
103- juice= asiir 104- knife= sikiin 105- know= ya'rif
106- ladder= daraj 107- land= ard (arz) 108- line= khat

Arabic

109- local= mahallii 110- loss= fiqdaan= khasaara
111- loud= aalin 112- love= hub= yuhib 113= low= munkhafid
114- lunch= ghidhaa(qaza) 115- market= suuq
116- mat (on floor) sajaada 117- mayor= muhaafiz
118- mean= yanii 119- meat= lahm 120- new= jadiid
121- mouth= fam 122- monkey= qird 123- money= nuquud
124- nose= anf 125- nuts= fustuq
126-okay= naam 127- open= maftuuh 128- page= safha
129- pane= lawh 130- pan= miqlaat 131- pen= galam
132- password = kalimat-al- ser 133- people= naas
134- pills, tablets= hubuub 135- playing cards = al waraq
136- pond= birka 137- potato= bataatis 138- photo= suura(sorat)
139- pulse= nabd(nabz) 140- pure= naqii 141- rain= ma tar
142-raw= khaam 143- really= haqqan 144- red= ahmar
145- scales= mizaan 146- shoe= hidhaa(hiza) 147- shop= yatasawwaq
148- sleep= yanaam 149- size= hajm 150- walk= mashie imshi

Russian

1-Good morning= Dobroye o'tra 2- good day= Dobry dyen'
3-good evening = dobry vyecher 4- hello= zdrgstvooeetye
5-goodbuy= Da sveedanya 6- I am called= Minya zavoot
7- please to meet you = Ochen preey atna
8-what are you called= Kak vas zavoot? 9 How are things= Kak dyila?
10-good well= Kharasho 11- excuse me/ I'am sorry= eezveeneetye maladoy
12- you= Vy 13- no= nyet 14- I = ya 15- not= nye 16- yes= Da
17- young woman/ miss= Dyevushka 18- we= Mbi 19- He= Oh
20-I don't understand = Yan ye paneemayoo
21- slower please= Myedlyn- ye- ye- pazhal- sta
22- I speak Russian badly= Ya gavaryoo pa- roosky plokha
23- you(several persons) = Bbi 24- She= Oha' 25- you= Tbi (1 person)
26- I= R> (R in other direction) 27- over there= von tam
28- cinema= keenotigtr 29- information office= spragvuchnoye
30- don't mention it= nye za shto! 31- c sound like s in sit
32- p sound like r in rabbit 33- e sound like ye = in yesterday
34- b sound like v in =visitor 35- h sound like n in = note
36-y sound like oo in boot 37- co'yc= savce (sound)
38- kakao= cacoa 39- rum= pom 40- sugar= caxap
41- red= krasny 42- white= byely 43- yellow= zholty
44- green= zilyony 45- black= chorny 46- go= eedeetye
47- how do you set to the center= kak papast v---? T sentr
48- straight a head= pryam ei 49- interesting= intiryesny
50- closed= zakryt
51=for repairs= na rimont 52- oh what a pity= kak zhal
53- aim= tsel 54- a live= zhivoy 55- all= vyes 56- angry= sirdity
57- art= isku'stva 58- ask= sprashivat, prasit 59- back= spina
60- bag= su'mka, mishok 61- bath= vana 62= bed= kravat
63- beer= piva 64- begin= nachinati 65- believe= palagat

66- best= luchshiy 67- bicycle= vilasipyet 68- blue= galuboy
69- blood= krof 70- born= razhdyony 71- bowl= miska
72- boy= malchik 73- brake= tarmazit 74- brand= fabrichnaya marka
75- bread= khlyep
76- bright= yarkly 77- brother= brat 78- build= stroyit
79- burn= zhar- azhok 80- bus= aftobus 81- butter= masla
82- cake= pirok 83- car= mashyna 84- care= zabota
85- careful= astarozhny 86- carpet= kavyo'r
87- chair= stul 88- cheap=dishovy 89- cheese= syr
90- chess= shakhmaty 91- chicke= ku'ritsa
92- child= ribyonok 93- choice= vybor 94- choose= vybirat
95- Christmas= razhdyestvo 96- circus= tsyrk
97- citizen= grazhdanin 98- city= go'rat 99- clean= chisty
100- clock= chisy
101- client= kliyent 102- closet= shkaf 103- clothes= adyezhda
104- cloud= oblaka 105- compare= sravnivat 106- cool= prakhladny
107- condition= usloviye 108- consist= sastayat'
109- cost= tsina 110- cow= karova 111- craft= rimislo'
112- crazy= sumashedshy 113- crime= pryestuplyeniye
114- culture= kultura 115- cut= paryes, 116- cat= ryezat
117- dad= papa 118- dairy(story) malochny magazine
119- danger= apasnast 120- dead= myortvy
121- decide= risha't' 122- divorce= razvod
123- drawing= risunok 124- excellent= privaskhodny
125- fabric= t kan'
126- fire= agon 127- fly= lit'at 128- god= bok
129- give= davit 130- hello= zdrastvuytye
131-Hole= dyra 132- home= dom 133- honesty= chyesny
134- hungry= galo'dny 135- husband= muzh 136- write= pisat
137- Conlibiac= loaf of fish, meat or vegetable baked in pastry shell.
138-Medovukha= A Russian honey, based alcoholic beverage
139- Okroshka= A type of Russian cold soup with mixed raw vegetable 140- Shchi= A type of Cabbage soup
141-Babushka= Grand mother , granny or just old woman
142-Inteligensia= Intelligence
143- Duma- To think, or to consider
144-Chlysty= Christ- belivers, Christianity
145-Bespopovtsy= Old believers.
146-Dosaaf= Free will or Valuntary, Navy, Military
147-Banya= Steam bath
148-Bylina= Occurred
149-VodKa= A 40% alcoholic liquor
150- Burlak= homeless

Greek

1-Hello= Kheh- reh-the 2- goodbue= yah sahs 3- yes= neh

4-ok= ehn- dah- ksee 5- no== oh khee 6- I'd like= thah-ee theh- lah

7-How much= Poh-soh 8- where is= Poo ee neh

9-Please= Pah- rah-kah-loh 10- Excuse me= Pah- rah-kah-loh

11- you are welcome= pah- rah-kah- loh

12-could you seak more slowly= hoh- ree-the- nah-mee-lah-the-pioh-ahr-ghah

13- I don't understand= thehn- kah-tah-lah-veh-noh

14- do you speak Greek? Mee-lah- the ahn gklee- kah

15- where is the restroom= poo-ee-neh ee too oh leh tah

16- Help=voh-ee-thee-ah 17- I'am just passing through= ohp-lohs pehr-nah-ah-poh-eh thoh

18-I have nothing to declare= Thehneh-khoh-nah-thee-loh-soh-tee-poh tah

19-customs= the-loh-nee-oh 20- duty free goods= ah-foh-roh-loh-yee-tah-ee thee

21-age= seem-foh-noh 22- air conditioning= Klee- mah – teez- mohs

23- animal= zoh-oh 24- arm= kheh-ree 25- art= tekh-nee

26- baby= moh-roh 27- baggage= ah-pohs- keh- yehs

28- bakery= ah- rtoh-pee-ee-oh 29- bank= trah-peh-zah

30- blind= peh- rsee- thels 31- boot= boh-tah 32- body= soh-mah

33- bowel= ehn- deh-roh 34- boxing= bohks 35- boy= ah-ghoh-ree

36- bridge= yeh-fee-rah 37- brush= voor – tsah

38- build= ktee-zoh 39- building= ktee-ree-oh

40- burn= eh- gah-mah 41- bus stop= stah-see-leh oh foh-ree-oo

42- butcher shop= kreh-oh- poh-lee-oh 43- café= kah-feh-the-ree-ah

44- bed room= eep-noh-thoh-mah-tee-oh

45- blood= eh-mah 46- broom= skoo-pah

47- business= bee znehs 48- call= klee-see

49- complain= pah-rah-poh-nieh-meh 50- computer= ee-poh-loh-yee-stees

51- condom= proh-fee-tah-ktee-koh 52- cancer= kahr-kee-nohs

53- court house= thee-kahs-tee-ree-oh 54- crown= koh-roh-nah

55- cup= flee-jah-nee 56- damage= zee-miah

57- dangerous= eh-pee-keen-thee-nohs 58- degrees= vohth-mee

59- delicious= nohs-tee-mohs 60- dentist= oh thohn-dee-ah-trohs
61- doctor= yah-trohs 62- diving= kah-tah-thee-tee
63- direction= oh thee- yee-ah 64- door= pohr-tah
65- divorced= thee-ah- zehv-ghmeh- nohs
66- drink= poh-toh-pee-noh 67- easy= ehf- koh-lohs
68- eat= troh-oh 69- example= pah-rah-theegh-mah
70- exit= eh-ksoh-thohs 71- fabric= ee-fahs-mah
72-face= proh- sah-poh 73- fall= pehf-toh
74- fan= ah-neh-mees-tee-rahs 75- far= mahk-ree-ah
76- fat= pah-khees 77- favorite= ah-ghah-pee-meh-nohs
78- ear= ahf-tee 79- feed= tah-ee-zoh 80- finger=thakh-tee-loh
81- fire= foh-tiah 82- fire escape= eh-ksoh-thohs keen-thee-noo
83- first class= proh-tee theh-see 84- flat= eh-pee-peh- thohs
85-flood= plee-mee-rah 86- flower=loo-loo-thee
87- fly= peh- tah-eh 88- foreign= Kseh-nohs
89- free= eh-lehf-theh-rohs 90- fresh= frehs-kohs
91- friend= fee-lohs 92- from= ah-poh 93-gift= thoh-roh
94- girl= koh-ree-tsee 95- glass= poh-tee-ree
96- glove= ghahn-dee 97- gold= khree- sohs
98- go= pee-yeh-noh 99- Greece= eh-lah-Thah
100- Hair= mah-liah
101- half= mee-sohs 102- hand= kheh-ree 103- hat= kah-peh-loh
104- handle= poh-meh-loh 105- hospital= noh-soh-koh-mee- oh
106- illegal= pah-rah-noh-mohs 107- illness= ahr-ohs-tee-ah
108- injection= eh-neh-see 109- injured= trahv-mah-teez-meh-nohs
110- invitation= prohs-klee-see 111- iron= see- theh roh
112- insurance= ahs-fah-lee-ah 113- jacket= sah-kah-kee
114- jar= yah-zoh 115- jaw= sah-ghoh-nee 116- knife= mah-kheh-ree
117- laugh= yeh-loh 118- library= veev-lee-oh-thee-kee
119- loose= fahr-thees 120- lotion= loh-siohn
121- loud= thee-nah-tohs 122- love= ah- ghah- poh
123- lunch= meh-see – mehr-yah-noh
124- main= kee-ree-ohs 125- map= khahr- tees
126- massage= mah-sahz 127- message= mee-nee-mah
128- metal= meh-tah-loh 129 –mobile phone= kee-nee-toh
130- money= khree-mah-tah 131- must= preh-pee
132- move= meh-tah-koh-mee-zoh 133- mouth= stah-mah
134- narrow= steh-nohs 135- name= oh-noh-mah
136- old= pah-liohs 137- old-fashioned= deh- mohn- deh
138- once= miah-foh- rah 139- paper= khar-tee
140- paint= zohgh-rah-fee-zoh 141- permit= ah-thee-ah
142- pickup= pehr-noh 143- police= ah-stee-noh-mee-ah
144- quiet= ee-see-khohs 145- ready= eh-tee-mohs

146- right= soh-stohs 147- river= poh-tah-mohs
148- snow= khioh-nee-zee 149- south= noh-tee-ohs
150- wrong= lah-thohs

Hindi

1-Go straight= see-de-joa-o 2- cheap ticket= sas-taa-tiket
3-a man= ek/ ko- ee- aad-mee 4- I = mayng 5- you= too
6-you are= hay 7- they= vo= hayng 8- he is British- Voh-an-grez hay
9-This room is full= yeh kam raa ba rea hay
10-this hotel= yeh hotal 11- those ones= voh
12- what's that= voh kyaa hay 13- how much does this coat cost= is kot kaa daam kyaa hay
14- she works= voh kam kar tee hay 15- she doesn't work= voh kam no beeng kar tee
16- could you please= me-har-baa-nee-kar ke
17-what time is it= Ta aim kyaa hay 18- what date is today= aaj kyaa toa-reek-hay
21-Spring= vas ant 20- summer= gar-mee ke din
21-autumn= pat-jar 22- winter= sar dee 23- week= is hafte
24- year= issaal 25- yesterday = kal
26- which…goes to (Karachi kaun-see (ka- roa) Chee= Jaa tee hay
27- first= Peh-lee 28- next= ag-lee 29- last= aaki-ree
30- Is this seat available= Kyaa yeh seet kaa lee hay
31- my luggage= me- raa-saa – man 32- duty free shop= dyee tee free
33- gate= get (teen) 34- please go straight to this address= is ee ja gah to fan ran jaa i- ye
35- I feel like going to a = jaa ne kaa man ra haa hay .
36- café= kay fe 37- party= paar- tee 38- I don't take drugs= mayng ne- shee-lee da von oag kaa
39- do you have a light= maa- chis hay 40- religion= maz-hab
41- I am not religious = me – raa- ka ee maz hab na heeng hay
42- catholic= kay to lik 43- Christian= ee- saa-ee
44- hindu= bin-doa 45- muslim= musal maan 46- sikh= sik
47- jewish= jayn 48- zoroastian= paar-see
49- cultural differences= Threani- akhtelaf
50- I 'm sorry, It is against my …… maaf kee ji-ye- yeh me re ke-vi rud hay.
51- I didn't mean to do/say any thing wrong= maaf kee ji ye jaan booj kar mayng nen yeh ha heeng ki yaa/ka haa.
52- shortest= cho-taa 53- toilets= taa-I – let
54- showers= na-haa-ne kee 55- cold= tand 56- hot= ba- hut- gar-mee
57- snowing= barf par- rahee 58- sunny= doop 59- warm= gar-mee

60- season= kaa-mau sam 61- flood= se-laab 62- dry= soo-kaa
63- animal= joan- var 64- flower= pool 65- plant= puu-daa
66- tree= per 67- breakfast= noash-tea 68- lunch= din-kaa-kaa-naa
69- to eat= kaa- naa 70- to drink= pee- naa
71- bar= ek baar 72- restaurant= res to rent 73- bill= bil
74- menu= men-yoo 75- God= Khoda
76- what would you recommend= aap ke kyat meng kyaa ach chaa ho gaa
77- breads= ro tee naan 78- soup= soups 79- salt= na mak
80- vinegar= sirkaa 81- spicy= ba- hut tee kaa 82- oily= ba hut tel
83- I'd like it= mu- je chaa hi ye 84- boiled= ab- laa
85- fried= ta-laa 86- medium= kam-pa kaa 87- steamed= baapse
88- well done= ach chee ta rah pa kaa 89- fire! Aaq
90- hot water= garm-paa-nee 91- water= paa – nee
92 a bottle of …. Wine= sha raab kee bo-tal
93- excuse me = su – ni – ye 94- beef= gosht
95- same again, please= va – hee-pitse dee ji ye 96- less= kam
97- what's the local specialty = kaas lo kal cheet kyaa hay
98- I'd like= mu- je… chaa- hi- ye 99- dairy products- ba-nee- chee-zong
100- garlic= lah- sun
101- fish= mach-lee 102- eggs= an-de 103- onion= pyeaz
104- thief= chor 105- go a way! Joa- o 106- watch out= ka- bar- daar
107- it's an emergency= I – mar- jen- see- hay
108- wallet= ba-tu-aa 109- I didn't do it= mayng ne na heeng ki you
110- I 'm sick= mayng bee maar hoong 111- heart attack= dil kaa dour aa
112- I feel dizzy= chak- kar-aa- ra – baa hay- 113- I have= mu- je.. hay
114- massage= malish 115- drug= ba- nee-da- vaa
116- salts= saalts 117- I have a cavity= ek daant meng ched hay
118- a board= savaar 119- gay= kosh 120- go= jaa-naa
121- good= ach- chaa 122- half= aa- daa 123- hire= ki raa ye par le naa
124- job= nouk-ree 125- marry= shad- dee= kar – naa
126- name= naam 127- now= ab 128- old= pu-raa- naa
129- open= kulaa 130- soon= jal- dee= early= fast
131- souvenir= ni- shaa- nee 132- spring= ba-haar
133- stop= lehr- naa 134- T.V = lee vee 135- vacant= kaa-lee
136- warm= garm 137- write= likh-naa 138- dark= daam
139- toothache= dant meng dard 140- chaa koo= knife
141- dirty= gan-daa 142- expensive= shob-doh
143- small= choh-toh 144- shoes= ju-ta
145 – I 'll think about it = chin-ta – koh- re – nay
146 – how much is it= e ta k otoh 147-what's that= oh-ta ki
148-what's your phone number= aap-nar fohn nom bohr ki
149- I 'd like to see = aa- mi… dek – te chai
150-

Southwest Black Bean Burgers

Prep Time
0
hr.
20
min.
Total Time
0
hr.
31
min.

Servings

6 servings

You don't have to be a vegetarian to enjoy this flavorful burger, made with black beans, salsa and chopped fresh cilantro.

What You Need

- 1/4 cup dry bread crumbs
- 3 Tbsp. KRAFT Real Mayo Mayonnaise
- 1 tsp. ground cumin
- 1/4 tsp. ground red pepper (cayenne)
- 2 cans (15 oz. each) black beans, rinsed, divided
- 2 stalks celery, finely chopped
- 1/4 cup chopped fresh cilantro
- 6 KRAFT Singles
- 6 whole wheat hamburger buns
- 6 lettuce leaves
— 1 ea For $1.49 thru 03/01
- 1/3 cup TACO BELL® Thick & Chunky Salsa
- 1/3 cup BREAKSTONE'S or KNUDSEN Sour Cream

Make It

- Use pulsing action to process bread crumbs, mayo, seasonings and half the beans in food processor until well blended. Transfer to large bowl; mix in celery, cilantro and remaining beans. Shape into 6 (1/2-inch-thick) patties.
- Cook in skillet sprayed with cooking spray on medium-high heat 5 min. on each side or until done (160ºF). Top with Singles; cook 1 min. or until melted.
- Fill buns with lettuce, cheeseburgers, salsa and sour cream.

Brazilian(Portuguese)

1-A lot= Mutio 2- accident= acidente 3- achieve,to= conse guir
4- Action= acao 5- actress= atriz 6- address= endereco
7- answer= the phone, = a tender telephone 8- any= qualquer
9-arrest= prender 10- art= arte 11- artist= artista
12- at the same time= mesmo tempo
13- attack= ataque 14- aunt= tie 15- bad= ruim 16- bag= bolsa
17- baggage= bagagem 18- bald= careca 19- bath= banho
20-beautiful= lindo, linda 21- beef= camedeboi 22- beer=cerveja
23- blind= cego 24- blond= louro, loura 25- blue= azul
26- book= livro 27- both= ambos, ambas 28- bread= pao
29- bride= noira 30- couple= casal 31- cousin(f)= prima
32- cousin(m)= primo 33- cultural= cultura
34- crime= crime 35- dentist= exigir 36- dial tone= sinal
37- dish= prato 38- divided= dividido 39- drunk= bebado
40- easy= facil 41- egg= ovo 42- embassy= embaixada
43- engineer= engenheiro 44- enjoy to= curtir
45- error= mistake= arro 46- escape= fuga
47-Excellent= excelente 48- excited= animado
49- sorry= comlicenca 50- exist to= haver
51- facing, in, - front of= defronte de 52- fast= rapido
53- factory worker= operario (m) operaria(f)
54- famous= Famoso ,= famosa 55- father= pai 56- frog= sapo
57- garage= garagem 58- get to= conseguir 59- give to= dar
60- go out= (leave to) = sair 61- go to bed= deitar- se
62- God= deus 63- good= boa-bom 64- good luck= boa sorte
65- grammar= gramatica 66- handset= gancho
67- hangover= ressaca 68- happy= contente- feliz 69- he= ele
70- heart= coracao 71- hello= alo 72- help= Socorro
73- her= dela 74- him self= si 75- hot= calor

76- hour= hora 77- house= casa 78- how many= quantos- or quantas
79- how much= quanto- quanta 80- hug= abraco 81-humor= humor
82= hunt= caca 83- hasband= marrido 84- idea= ideia
85- identical= identico 86- illegal= ilegal 87- insistence= insistencia
88- instructor= instrutor 89- intelligent= inteligente
90- inventor= inventor 91- Iranian= iraniano
92- Iraq= Iraque 93- Israel= Israel 94- Judge= juiz= juiza
95- key= chave 96- king= Rei 97- kiss= beijo
98- lesson= licao 99- liberty= Liberdade 100= liqueur= licor
101-lose to= perder 102- love= amar 103- may= poder
104- melon= melao 105- merry chrismas= Feliz natal
106-message= recado 107- milk= leite 108- mirror= espelho
109- miserable= miseravel 110- miss to = fezer falta
111- moment= momento 112- paid= pago 113- pencil= lapis
114-perfume= perfume 115- people= gente
116- personal= infinitive 117- paper= papel
118- park= parquet 119- party= festa 120- pass, to= passer
121- pen= caneta 122- pay, to = pagar 123- peach= pessego
124- pediatrician= pediatra 125- persistent= persistente
126- physical= fisico 127- pig's ear= orelha de porco
128- pilot= piloto 129- place= lugar 130- planet= planeta
131- play= jogar 132- pleasure= prazer 133- pity= do'
134- raw= cru- crua 135- reflect to= reflector
136- remembrance= lembranca 137- reptile= reptile
138- rice= arroz 139- rifle= fuzil 140- said= ditto
141- salt= sal 142- same= mesmo 143- school= escola
144- she= ela 145- sick= doente 146- single= solteiro
147- sister= irma' 148- sleep to = dormer
149- talent= talento 150- tree= arvore

Mushroom and Epazote Tacos

- Yield: 6 servings
- Prep Time: 5-10 minutes
- Cook Time: 3-4 minutes

Mushroom and Epazote Tacos

Ingredients

- Guerrero® Yellow Corn Tortillas - 12
- Vegetable oil - 4 Tablespoons
- Button mushrooms - 2 Cups, sliced
- Poblano peppers - 2, roasted, peeled and cut into strips
- White onion - 1, cut into strips
- Epazote - 2 Tablespoons, washed and chopped
- Sour cream - ½ Cup
- Cacique® queso fresco - ¼ Cup
- Sea salt
- Pepper

Instructions

1. In a medium size skillet, heat the oil over high heat and add the onions; cook until translucent, add the mushrooms and poblano peppers. Cover and let it cook for 3-4 minutes.
2. Add the epazote and season with salt and pepper. Add the sour cream and mix in. Remove from the heat and set aside.
3. Warm tortillas on a hot comal, fill with them with the creamy mushrooms, top with queso fresco and enjoy

Turkish

1-Gu'zel= beautiful, 2- gu'zellik= beauty 3- mutlu= happy
4- mutluluk= happiness 5- iyi= good 6- iyilik=goodness
7- zor= difficult 8- zorluk= difficulty
9-kiz arkadasimin mutluugu mu kendi mutlulugumdan daha o'nemlidir?
= is my girlfriend's happiness more important than my own happiness?
10-gu'zelligine= its beauty (gu'zel-lig-i-n-e)
11-su manzaranin gu'zelligne bakin! = regard the beauty of this view!
12-zorluklarimiz= our difficulties
13- tabi bu zorluklarimiz oldu oma hicbir zaman bu zorluklarimizdan yilmadik! = we are subject to difficulties, but we have never been afraid of our difficulties!
14- baba= father 15 babacik= daddy
16- kedi= cat 17- kediciki= pussy cat
18- ko'pek= dog 19- ko'pecik= puppy
20-otobu's hat ve gu'zergahlari kitapcigi= auto bus line and routes booklet.
21-hosgeldin arkadascigim! = welcome my dear friend!
22-ku'cu'k= small 23- ku'cu'cu'k= little
24- ufak= small ufacik= tiny, minute
25-minik= small and nice
26-minicik= wee, tiny 27- az= less 28- azicik= little less
29-as in birazicik= just a little
30- bir= one 31- biricik= unique
32- dar= narrow 33- daracik= narrowish
34-im= my 35- baba cigim= my daddy
36- ko'pecigim!= my little puppy
37- genc= young 38- genclik= youth
39- yasli= old 40- yaslilik the aged
41- insan= person 42- insanlik= humam-kind
43- kisi= person/individual 44- kisilik= personality/ identity
45- bakan= minister 46- bakanlik ministry
47- bakanligi= ministry of justice

48- balik= fish 49- balikci= fisherman
50- balikcilik= fishing club, group, association
51- tuz=salt 52- tuzluk= salt cellar
53- biber= papper 54- biberlik = peper shaker
55- go'z= eye 56- go'zlu'k= spectacles
57- kira= hire 58- kiralik= for hire
59- yagmur= rain 60- yagmurluk= rain coat
61- bakanlik binasi= ministry building
62- camasir= laundry
63- camasirlik= laundry room
64- bahce= rock garden 65- orman= forest
66- ormanlikalan= forested area
67- o ormanda cok yabani hayvan varmis = it seems there are many wild animals in that forest.
68- elmalik= apple orchard 69- elma= apple
70- sebzelik= vegetable garden 71- sebze= vegetable
72- ciceklik= flower garden 73- cicek= flower
74- kitaplik= book case 75- kitab= book
76- on yumurta= ten eggs 77- sabir= patience
78- on yumurtalik bir kutu istiyorum.= I want a ten eggs
79- iki kisilik cadir var mi?= is there a tent of two person? Double tent."
80- evet var. kac gu'nlu'k?= yes there is . how many days?
81- sabirsiz= impatient 82- dikkat= care 83- dikkatsiz= careless
84- kapinin zili= the door bell (kapi-nin- zil-i)
85- isik diregi= lamp post 86- ali nin elma agaci= ali's apple tree.
87- deniz suyu= the sea water 88- Kadin dektoru= lady doctor.
89- otobu's duragi= bus stop 90- police car= polis orabasi
91- meyve suyu= fruit juice 92- et suyu= gravy
93- elma suyu= apple juice 94- pinar suyu= spring water
95- cep telefonlari= mobil phone 96- tahta kapi= wooden door
97- camasir makineleri= washing machines
98- demir ko'pru'= iron bridge
99- odada= in the room 100- nakit= cash
101-Yatakta= on the bed 102- masada= from the table
103- cevaptan= from the answer
104- c,ay pahali= tea is expensive 105- banka= bank
106- cay soguk= the tea is cold 107- og'ul= from the son
108- araba caddede= the car is in the road
109- adam kapiyi= the man closed the door
110- fikir= idea 111- kutu= box 112- evim= my house
113- evimi= my house 114- adam kilidimi= the man locked.
115- kilid – im– i.=my lock 116- agizda= in the mouth
117- keyif= joy 118- beyinden= from the brain
119- isimim = my name 120- kayiptan= from the loss

Ayran with Mint , or Yoguort drink

This is very similar to plain Ayran. However, mint is added to provide refreshing taste during hot summers of Anatolia.

Ingredients:

- 1 pint plain yogurt (the thicker the better)
- Several ice cubes
- A generous pinch of salt
- A little chopped fresh mint
- 1 pint water

How to prepare:

1. Add yogurt and water to a blender.
2. Add ice cubes and salt. Add a bit of fresh mint, optional.
3. Blend until well mixed.
4. Serve.

Ayran with Mint

References:

New Testament Greek
Japanese in plain English
Beginner's Russian
Book bridges for ESL students
Beginner's French dictionary
Barron's E_Z Spanish
Berlitz Greek phrase book
Chinese
English for coming Americans

Essential Arabic : speak Arabic
Easy Russian phrase book
English through the ages
Italian in 10 minutes
Instant German
Learn French
Spanish the easy way
Side by side Italian & English grammar
Hindi Urdu & Bengali
Teaching English as a second language
Teach yourself Hindi dictionary
The everything Brazilian Portuguese Phrase.

Cap Economy for Saving the World

By Majid Khodabandeh
2019

My name is Majid Khodabandeh

I am 60 years old, older than
Moses when he wrote the 10 commands, and I have a view of more than 6 thousand years history of the world with travelling and be in different continent, which most leaders in past didn't do it. All prophets just traveled only few cities. Also, prophets ridding with donkey. I am older than Jesus, who was only less than 36 years old with all his story and his issues, I am older than Mohammad which when he was died, he was around 60ths with all his story and his issues. I am older Karol Marcs, and Lenin with communist idea and new world on his time which everyone makes same wage or minimum wage with his idea and his issues. I am older than Gondi and his nationalism idea and his story and his issues.

    Also, I am older than all human being or statue or machine already they build it. All writers or story about statue build for several months like story of Buda or any handmade figures are fake. all those stories are fake with fake figure and fake news and all laws for those country made by human with lack of experience and knowledge of reality. Also, which those wisdom was less than 60 years old when the wrote his story and his, or her issues. I am, as a human being with long journey from Asia to Europe to America was brilliant experience with mazing learning experience which I want to share it to you all. Also, I believe you as a human being can be a prophet and perfect human being too. Like any history wrote so far, are fake news. there are all over the world they way history wrote are to manipulate the innocent people. we as human and some as a writer must be careful and not aggregate the writing which it is not reality and are not fact. Most writing in past were wrong news and aggregate feeling of writing too much, especially in religion point of view and using human magnesian or weakness to extra mile and give in the wrong news of fake news in today's language and daily life.

    During my life I saw and lived in Dictatorships countries, Socialism, Communist countries, I was in Capitalism, Kingdom, religion government countries. I studied Architecture, ant apology, social ology, geology, civil engineering, city planning, public admi. Laws, and business. I was self-employee, retail dealer psychology at work and social works and I, studies of human behavior, etc. at work and societies without any title. I did lean a lot and see all different political and social events and activities directly with actual peoples. I saw perfection and un perfection. I saw to many peoples goes up and so many people come down from power. I saw too many businesses open and close, too many government changes. I saw many changes in world from kingdom to socialism or dictatorship to commonest from capitalisms to socialism or kingdom to religion government. I saw changes from communism to religion. I saw communism ideology, or democratic or republic party which all they don't make sense after few years and all politician lost after a while. All politician who are someone looking for own pocket and run for political office, whom are not very nice and just talking and used one of the human senses which is speaking too much. politician elected by the people to take chairs and nothing do after they are in the office and just lie to public and used the sense of speaking too much. All those politician and people whom follow them look like it cannot make it right decision. Usually all politician or economist peoples with idea last for several years and people they get tired of those rules, after a while and wants to change again to new idea or different party, like depress house wife. Look like it Humanity needed always changing. But is reality human needed are never changed for those needs which are 5 things, food, home, transportation, love, and communication devises.

    If politicians follow this need, we have less problems in world we are we are good for future generation with those needs and safety for all. If people need more work done for basic needs, government which are new parents for all of human in the nation must take care of this important. All this needs they leave me a question for me If people ask for new reform or revolution or codetta can solve human needs, are those needs are obvious and we don't need revolution or get crazy reform or revolution. I asked again If these needs are in any country difference from USA or all those needs are all the same for all human being. if politician which is part of government must provide to all those basic needs is necessary to survival and make it comfortable for all humans. we as a human we must not go too far for all basic needs. To see unnecessary needs are is under question for committee of economy aspect and make good look of cities and neighborhood. We usually most the time we see, and we are going too far in wrong direction. we are thinking needs are endless for humans and luxury add in daily life. But all humans need, are just food and housing, love, transportation and communication devise. My Idea about Cap economy is very simple and easy to understand and is necessary to survive in today's world. Government can with this extra money for cap economy goes to satisfy all senses which is 9 senses and all human basic needs which is food, home, love, transportation and communication devices. We must like any organization we have so far control the wealth for humans and balance the humanity with wealth. We must somehow control and balance the wealth for people with laws and understanding of human behavior with psychology. one person cannot be going wild and take advantage to others for greed or wrong market un balance. we must look for human success and capital wealth with the vision and cap economy. To have cap for healthy economy we must for any position put cap to everybody as human equality and equal opportunity is the key to new world. We must have peace and equal humans balance wealth and even up the world with raise the men, and women. It is always good perfect human, with freedom to grow and explore to the highest point of humanity with freedom. good human is to have all freedom right to choose. We must protect all women and men, children, handicap, and older people etc. To have a vision and to see the limited world what we have and to share it, is the key point to survive in new world. we must share to be equal for basic needs. To have a cab economy in every position we must have a sense of equality with freedom and no one can take advantage of the other take more than they needed. To have equal opportunity we must balance thought and wealth for humanity. which we must have supreme cap economy job court. Supreme cap economy is for set of the wages for all jobs, gov., or privet, nonprofit or profit companies from regular labors to CPO. Or president or owner, or sport team. we must decide in this important issue. This cab economy still makes a capitalism and raise the humans in any phases and opportunity is endless for any job. For Example, like military person start for very basic major to all the way to general. Other example in grocery or retails we have cap for every position like meat cutter for example if it is 22.00 dollars per hours is the cap which usually after 3 years in the position they receive the 22 $ cap and after that no more raise is different department or different position with the new supreme economy cap provides to retails and all other businesses we must control the wealth. My idea is going to every job from top to the bottom even in sport and CPO and all manager and business owner or corporation everything effected. We must have a cap there are all nation and world wealth are in hand of committee and no one can exceed more than they needed. Which if human's greed is control, with set of the wealth, if wealth are not control it can be destroy freedom and others and one person or family or even nation can destroy the others or even world. If we don't have a control of the wealth, Humanities, small or big can be all kinds of dictatorship in small level or big level which can cause damage freedom and democracy. one person cannot have more than his or her needs. Cap economy control the wealth of all peoples. We as a one person vote to committee, which with cap economy we set of the wage they needed for that owner or labor's worker, him or her basic needs with even wealth. one they can't have mullite million dollars and someone cry for mercy. we must change this auditees for whole world with cap economy for freedom, safety, wealth and comfortable human being to satisfy all senses too and given basic needs to all.

Cap economy means what is highest paying in the nation person can make, like a minimum wage we have a maximum wage we have. Person cannot make more than maximum wage in private or government profit or nonprofit. which we must create committee which are 16 persons selected every 2 years by public for all jobs, from different businesses and different back ground we selected and with education and with experience make goal base on economy of the year set of the minimum wage and maximum wage. in any businesses we are we must set of the one-person wealth to control for safety of all, and protect the freedom. We must put the Cap for any person, like CPO maximum they can make for example is 1 million in the year. football player highest they can make 200,000.00 $a year. Owner of the business or businesses make 400,000.00$ for each business. President, or owner of the company can make up to 2 million. these are including all bonuses and extra money. cap economy is control person wealth to balance the world with freedom and capital also with grow of economy and wealth to everyone in world equality. In cab economy rest of the money and profit for company goes to cap investment for whole nation and this rest of the money from businesses goes to build a hospital or school or university, road and bridges, etc. To subsidized food and cars and homes for low income. This extra money is cap inv. And is extra from tax payer and we can lower taxes for people too, this cap inv. We Can pay student loan and health care to everyone. This extra budget from taxes and this extra money we can call it green budget, or cap investment.

This Cap Economy will balance the wealth for people with freedom and healthy economy which we can call it green budget. Also, will cause the businesses to add more money given to all other employees also created more middle class in world and less economy problems for all. Cap Economy is the key for healthy economy. I published the book" world language" which I discuses about 32 hours full time works for week job and add more money to employee's pocket or more hourly wages. what they were making for 40 house changes for same money for 32 hours works. To have Cap Economy which we must set of the committee and research continuing years after years for make a new decision based on economy which provide every year to any nations and will eventually make it global cap economy for world base of cost of living and living expenses and wealthy nation and wealthy world.

It is not healthy if economy like today's world to have only 400 people hold a 60% of the wealth of the country in USA and are poor must suffer, and it is not right. this 400 people take everything for them and is not right. All fortune 500 company look like it is like a kingdom goes to his son or his family, which are these wealth of businesses is not right that way and damage freedom and safety. we must look all those wealth is belonging to nation wealth and not company or person or family. Do wealth belong to nation. People invested to buy the computers or electronic or cloths or furniture's or homes or tools there are all people money must return to people the company created something which not Last, is come back to people. Money can be saved and endless life span, but merchandises are destroy or damage. which money is wealth of people and must share and build freedom and safety to all.

International Agriculture Cap Economy.

To have a view of the past to present and future of the world we learning to feed the public always is big responsibility to any nation which was in the past on solders of the farmers. In the new world farmer, are working for international agriculture which is part of government. we want to make agriculture more to be an organization and has an employee with international view of hunger and needs with variety of foods and healthy chooses to everyone.

To have a vision of the world with lands and vision of rains and climate we can send a motorize farm equipment to all over the world and our planet and grows fruits, grains, crops, frozen food and farm animals like chicken, turkey, caw, ships, pigs, fish etc., for every human been and no hunger anymore. Food they can sell it in market cheapest they can make and make subsidized some prices for necessary foods like bread, meats and cheeses, and vegetables, etc., and international agricultures are runs by government and they have employees not privet farmers. Framers works for government, and price of food control by government and committees and government is parents of all humans.

Every state has own agriculture organization and working with other nation which has a same climate. university professor and student that do the research and go travel and co-op in different country or in the state must build a housing in next to the farm land for engineering and students with equipment operator and regular labors workers. Employees are seasonal travelling and rotating students all the time and prevent suicide too. international agricultures group cultivating the croups and produce foods with a lot of employees and used military base too as an agriculture military. This service can be for students to pay student loan for 2 years which paid of student loans. Same for doctors and engineering, which are military doctors and nurses too. military engineering agricultures and doctors and nurses can be 2 years for student loan paid off the loan and service the publics. All employees we must pay all of them fairs with free food and housing during the mission. I recommended all student with research and close university watch and home works and learning from screech and move to the leadership and high pay with good retirement.

Building housing materials control and try to teach the people to builds own house.

Car factory and transportation cheapest can be with variety of chooses and with cap economy. Military engineers can work at car factory to bring the cost down and get car with lower cost.

Military doctor and nurses can bring the healthcare is lower they can or free healthcare for all, with 2 years minimum wages as a co-op and will paid off the student loan too with building the government hospitals, and clinic, with free services. This can be achieved with free money from cap economy or green investment.

How wrong religion or faith can direct the economy in wrong direction or fake economy are must be watch carefully.

We must consider faith is imaginary and not reality. to believe on god and having some imaginary love or faith make a economy imaginary and fake too. We must go with reality and with science.

Prevent any fake economy specially with cap economy we must look everything year to years and go with reality of life. History as I told you in my book, legal concept of the law and human behavior senses has a lot of wrong story. I said in my book Most of Story of geneses in old testimony and Koran or Tora are wrong story and all this follower can have created wrong messages or fake economy. philosophy of communists is wrong too or Buda wrong too. Usually in world still teach in school story of Noah and world was flooded and to not knowing in Noah time, world was not discovering was round and goes around sun which Galileo discovered only 500 years ago and Noah was 5 thousand years ago. In Noah time they may be was in Turkey or Afghanistan rained for several days they thought whole world was flooded and technology was not strong enough to carry 2 elephants, 2 Greif of all the other animal and your family in one ship no nails and no discovery of iron. ridding with donkey and no air planes. America was not discovered. There is other story like Adam and eve which they said Adam and eve were first humans, and philosophy were wrong if Adam was first human, he must sleep with her daughter or eve sleep with his son for more population. which are wrong story and wrong philosophy with they take an economy or cap economy in wrong direction. History must be with reality and day to day life, and no fake news like Jesus will come back to save you or Moses or Mohammad or Emmom zaman come back to save you and wrong news. People must understand of needs and what is reality of life and must work on it to make an economy strong and make a right decision. We must understand human life last for almost maximum 100 years not more and everyone will be dyeing eventually. To have a cap economy we have strong economy with equal opportunity and equal right with freedom and wealth also, healthy economy.

Communist are wrong economy too. in new world we as people must paid on experiences and education and they have choose making to any thought and job they like and wealth they needed. equal opportunity equal pay for women and men and with freedom. Only economy we used they have a cap for any jobs and businesses, bosses or owners of businesses we must with committee choose the wages and income for everyone. Board of cap economy which has a research center and committee work on set up income of businesses and make a cap for any jobs or corporation or businesses and control by the peoples chooses with freedom of constitution branch of government.

Socialism Economy is wrong too. in socialism countries or idea, we see government take money as a tax too much to pay for roads school, hospitals, etc. From middle class, which middle class right now in those countries are poor right now and struggling for bills and basic needs. Those countries take away money from middle class and too much taxes. Socialism make is somehow to pay unemployment people or handicap or older people a little bit which is not right economy. We must in new world everyone somehow works and control the wealth and activities. Cap economy makes money and helps the economy in capital world and humans are capital investment. We must create for even everyone works at home or any organization we must create the job or assignment weekly for few hours to full time as assignment to be any life. I wrote this book to promote the freedom and equal humanity to everyone with the vision of to grow with capitalism with the cap economy to save the world for generation after generation. no one can take advantage from others. If someone works hard, and studies hard get experience and knowledge can be raise to the top of the company or communities or cities or even countries.

We must have learned all humans senses, which human has 9 senses and to satisfy those human senses is parity and we have perfect human being. to satisfy all senses we must change the laws and psychology base on those senses with equal opportunities to everyone and equal human being with freedom and freedom to choose and open minded to cap economy.

Summery"

Cap Economy is solution economy for new world and every person must have a cap income which set up by committee and humans needs are parity which are needs of foods and homes, loves, communication, and transportation. government responsible to all nation.

And government is mother and father of all human of any nation.

we must have learned human has 9 senses and we will change the human psychology and laws base on human has 9 senses which are senses vision, hearing, smelling, testing, relief, sexuality, speaking, and senses of love or hate or senses of telepathy or soul.

I hope this book open door to all human being in world for freedom and all needs with equal pay and safety to all. Thanks again with kindest regards MAJID KHODABANDEH

11/22/2019
MASON , OHIO , USA

www.ingramcontent.com/pod-product-compliance
Lightning Source LLC
Chambersburg PA
CBHW042358030426
42337CB00032B/5147